RARITY OF HYBRID AND DIFFICULTY OF BREEDING

No. 1 is the easiest – No. 6 is the hardest

1	
2	
3	
4	
5	
6	
Not yet done	

British Birds

Mules and Hybrids

Bernard Williams

2006

First published in England in 2006 by B.C. Williams
85 Northwood Lane, Clayton, Newcastle under Lyme, Staffordshire ST5 4BN

www.bcwilliams.co.uk

Printed in Wales by Gwasg Gomer, Llandysul

ISBN 0-9554037-0-7
978-0-9554037-0-5

British Library Cataloguing in Publication Data
A catalogue record for this book is available from the British Library.

CONTENTS

Canary × crossbill family

ACKNOWLEDGEMENTS

Many people have contributed to the publication of this book. Firstly, my father, who has been a constant support and encouragement since I was a boy. He has always shown an interest in my bird keeping activities and has always been there to talk to me, even when no one else was interested. Now well into his 70s, he is still the person with whom I have most in common. It is great to have a father who has also been a best mate.

Much of the time, while I was writing this book, my late mother has been close to my thoughts as I remembered times gone by. Amongst many other things, she helped with the catering at all the shows with which I was involved. Sometimes she cooked more than 100 three-course meals for stewards, judges and visitors.

Always at the front of my mind are my wife Susan and children Christopher and Sarah, who have put up with so much. Being part of a bird keeping family can be difficult at times; never being able to go out for the day until the birds have been fed. Whenever I have been ill they have taken over the bird room duties. Perhaps worse for them has been having to put up with my passion and listening to my constant ramblings about my breeding failures and all the politics in the hobby that have cropped up over the years.

I thank Roy Stringer, a good friend for the last 25 or more years. His help and advice during the preparation of this book have been invaluable. I am grateful to Tony Tilford for his kindness in granting permission for the free use of many of the pictures. I also thank Mrs Avon for providing some of the photographs taken by her late husband, Dennis Avon.

I am grateful to *Cage & Aviary Birds* magazine for a selection of photographs and especially to Editorial Administrator, Lynn Sullivan, for her personal assistance. Roger Caton and Bill Doherty have both provided welcome advice and help. Ron Phillips kindly allowed me to use information from his book, *The History of the Scottish British Bird and Mule Club* and both he and Bertrand Stengs helped with photos.

I would finally like to thank *Alcedo Ornitologia e Natura* of Italy (http://www.alcedoedizioni.it/) for the use of linnet × crossbill hybrid photos.

B. C. Williams
October 2006

FOREWORD

It is some years now since a book on British hybrids was written by an expert in the field and, in my opinion, the time is ripe for this new offering. As Features Editor of *Cage & Aviary Birds* I have been fortunate enough to get to know, and become friends with, the authors of this book's predecessors; Walter Lewis, Victor Carr, Peter Lander and Bob Partridge: every one of them a world expert. So it is fitting that this new book has been written by Bernard Williams, a man who is just as well qualified as those already named.

The text and illustrations are impressive. The text brings much of what has been written in the past up to date and the illustrations are unsurpassed in their quality and inventiveness. Until now hybrids have never been viewed in this way.

It is not only the people who breed British birds and hybrids who take an interest in our native birds. So it is not just these specialists who will gain from reading this book.

I recommend it to the breeders and keepers of all types of birds.

Roy Stringer

Crossbill × bullfinch family

INTRODUCTION

Hybridising offers a challenge completely different to any other sort of bird breeding. This is because the birds produced are infertile and, generally speaking, there is only one chance of success. By contrast, breeders of British birds, canaries, budgerigars and foreign birds can build and improve on a successful bloodline. In those branches of the fancy, very skilful breeders can produce related winners year after year.

To try to improve the results from a hybridising pair you could select different mates for the parent birds but there is every chance that the new pairings will be incompatible and no young will be produced. Although some hybrids are easier to breed than others, none is as easy as breeding from birds of the same species. To breed good hybrids you need to be totally dedicated – or lucky.

That's the bad news. Now I can get on to the good news. Every year we see winning hybrids that have come from chance pairings. That's where the luck comes in. In fact, surprising as it may sound, hybrid breeding is a great branch of the hobby for aviculturists with limited experience. You could say that there are two types of hybrid breeder. First, there are experienced fanciers for whom hybridisation is an art. They turn out winners year after year. Then there is the novice who produces a top-class specimen out of the blue.

I cannot think of any other branch of bird keeping that gives every exhibitor the same chance of winning. What makes hybrid breeding even more attractive is that a first class hybrid is so eye-catching that it is capable of sweeping all before it on the show bench. The fact that they are unusual and not easy to breed gives hybrids the edge over even top-quality canaries and budgerigars. As a result, over the years we have seen certain hybrids come to the fore in taking the top awards.

For a good many years it was the canary × bullfinch, then

Unflighted yellow canary × crossbill cock

In this picture, the bird's tail and wings are not colour fed. Canaries, mules and hybrids do not moult their wing flights and tail until their first full moult at one year old, hence the term 'unflighted'. After this first-year moult, the tail and flight feathers match the rest of the body colour.

examples of redpoll × bullfinch, greenfinch × bullfinch and chaffinch hybrids tended to come out on top. But rarity is not everything. A good, dark goldfinch, greenfinch or linnet mule is always hard to beat. Mule and hybrid breeding is now a very specialist branch, but so are many other branches of the fancy. In the 35 years I have been actively involved with the hobby I have seen it decline, with the loss of more than 1,000 cage bird societies in the United Kingdom since 1980.

In 2003 and 2004, animal rights activists prevented the staging of the National Exhibition, a show with its origins in the mid 1800s. This history of over 160 years had previously only been broken by World War II and even then the war ran for six years and the show was suspended for only four. The passion is still there but the number of exhibitors has fallen. There still seem to be as many bird keepers although I believe the hobby is changing as the majority of people who keep birds do not exhibit them any more.

If you attend the large bird sales that are put on around the country you will see what I mean. The number of visitors seems to grow every year with as many as 5,000 people attending at some venues. Only the National Exhibition, with a regular attendance of 10,000, could attract more people to a single event. The largest events, for example the World Show, are now held in Europe. Such events are gigantic. The last continental event I attended was in Holland and the attendance was 26,000. This proves that there is still great interest in bird keeping.

But alas, even the World Show was cancelled in 2005, as were lots of our United Kingdom events, due to another problem. This time it was bird flu. Thankfully the restrictions were soon lifted so some events that looked as though they would have to be cancelled still took place.

I hope that the future brings us better fortunes. At the time of writing it looked as though the Animal Welfare Bill was set to remove all the ambiguity that has given the National Exhibition, and other major events, so much trouble over the previous five years. We must hope that bird flu doesn't take its place as a reason for limiting our activities. Nevertheless, the shows I have attended have still been as well supported as they ever were. It seems nothing will stop people enjoying one of the best hobbies around.

If there is one more thing I would like to do it would be to see another National Exhibition, the shop window of our hobby. This great event is probably responsible for more new bird keepers starting in the hobby than any other event. Taking place in December, it also creates a grand finale to the year for experienced fanciers and helps maintain their interest. The best and worst time I ever had in bird keeping was in 2004. In February of that year I was appointed show organiser for

Clear, buff goldfinch mule, twice Supreme Winner for Walter Jones

Lightly marked, goldfinch mule,
Supreme Winner for Oldknow and Brankin

the National Exhibition only to see the show cancelled just four weeks before the event was due to take place because of the activities of animal rights activists. After nine months of hard work and planning this was soul destroying. It was like building a house, putting on the last brick, moving all the furniture in and then being told to demolish it.

Since then, I feel many bird keepers have been cheated by these activists out of the awards which would have recognised their achievements. The Supreme Award at the National is the most coveted award in our hobby; the equivalent of Best in Show at Crufts. Fanciers spend a long time trying to breed a bird to win this award. During the last two years there have been birds bred that would have won, or would at least have stood a good chance of winning. Unfortunately they have been robbed of this chance by the activists who have prevented the National taking place.

Who knows how many more wonderful specimens will be bred and die without their breeders having a chance to be rewarded for a once in a lifetime achievement?

Presentation of the Supreme Award at the National Exhibition, 2002

The author
at the National Exhibition

MULES

Until canaries were brought to our shores, the only birds kept as pets, by the ordinary folk of Great Britain, would have been native finches. True, a few exotic birds, such as parrots were brought in by ocean-going mariners, but these were the province of only the very rich.

Ever since canaries arrived they have been crossed with most European finches to produce hybrids. The birds produced from canary × finch matings are commonly called mules because, almost without exception, they are infertile. The exceptions to the naming convention are the canary × bullfinch and canary × chaffinch which, by tradition, are referred to as hybrids.

The progeny of two finches of different species are called

Canary × crossbill buff cock
Crossbill hybrids are on Schedule 4, and should be rung and registered with DEFRA.

hybrids. In rare instances hybrids have been found to be fertile, so if you hear a bird referred to as a mule you know that one of its parents is a canary.

Most canary breeds are used in the production of mules. Which breed is most suitable depends upon what is required of the young, such as exhibition quality, song or colour. The best canary types for each category are the yellow Norwich for exhibition quality, the coloured canary for colour and the roller-type canary for song.

Yellow Norwich canary

EXHIBITION

If your aim is to exhibit and win top prizes on the show bench with mules, there is really only one canary that is suitable; the yellow Norwich. This canary, above all others, gives a desirable combination of size, shape and colour to mules.

Some breeders believe the best mules are bred from a Norwich cock paired with a finch hen. This may be true, but it is almost always more difficult to produce youngsters from this combination than from a finch cock mated with a Norwich canary hen.

Although canary hens generally go to nest in a cage more readily than finch hens, Norwich hens can be very poor at rearing young. So, if you breed mules from Norwich hens, foster parents are the best option.

Greenfinch hens rear well in cages, so using a Norwich canary cock with a greenfinch hen is a good bet. If the eggs are clear, try putting some full eggs from another pair under the greenfinch hen to double your chance of success.

To breed good mules consistently, you need a stud of quality Norwich canaries to produce a regular supply of yellow cocks and hens. You will also need various European finches and foster canaries already proven to be good feeders.

Only yellow Norwich canary mules should be shown, especially in the champion classes, as a good yellow mule will always beat a buff mule. Buff mules occasionally win in the novice section where the competition is not so fierce. But a champion buff mule needs to be a very special bird.

Evaluate all of the young mules you breed as a group. All the buff cocks and hens, and most of the yellow hens, can be disposed of and the final selection made from the remainder. It is impossible to use the mules you have bred to improve your stud the following year because of their infertility. To make improvements, the only option is to split up a pair and introduce a new mate for one or both, although this usually lessens the chance of the new pairs being compatible. When choosing the right Norwich from which to breed mules, always use full yellow green hens to reduce the chance of light feathers in your mules. Odd light feathers spoil a good mule and are faults when showing.

Linnet mules rarely have light feathers even when using clear canaries but goldfinch mules regularly show light feathers so always use dark birds for this cross. Dark canaries also make the mule's colours darker and well defined but cinnamon canaries reduce the definition making the black areas seem slightly greyer. Mule breeding for exhibition is very challenging. If your aim is to breed lots of birds then it is not for you. But if you like a challenge then no other branch of bird keeping is so rewarding.

COLOUR

In continental Europe the emphasis appears to be on the colour rather than the size of mules, even though Northern goldfinches which are larger but less colourful than British goldfinches are used most often. Coloured canaries, particularly red factors, produce the best range and depth of colour. Mules bred from coloured canaries can be shown in the miniature mule class but to succeed show only yellow-feathered cocks with very rich colour.

Colour feeding should start when a mule is six weeks old. All young birds moult their body feathers at this age but not their main flight, wing and tail feathers. These remain in place until their second year at which time every feather is moulted. For this reason the term 'unflighted' is applied to canaries and mules bred in the current year and 'flighted' to birds in their second year and

Red factor canary

beyond. Colour feeding is not at all difficult these days with products such as Carophyll Red and Canthaxathin. Colour food should be mixed in a small amount of boiling water 24 hours before use and then topped up with cold water until the mixture is a rich, red colour. This mixture should be offered instead of drinking water to mules and coloured canaries right through the moult. Do not stop until every feather has regrown.

Overfeeding colour food gives birds a burnt appearance, resulting in brownish instead of rich, red plumage. Red droppings are an indication of over colour feeding, so reduce the strength. Experience is the only way to judge the correct amount of colour food for a particular bird. Each bird's reaction to colour feeding may be slightly different as some feather types take colour better than others.

SONG

The original reason for cross breeding canaries with finches was to produce singing mules. If the young mules are housed away from canaries after weaning, and kept in earshot of their finch parent, the cocks sing almost pure finch song with just a trace of their canary origins. The mule hens are of no use other than as pets because of their lack of song and their infertility.

The best canary to use for singing mules is any of the roller type canaries as they have the widest range of notes and sweetest song. Such mules are much sought after.

Two finches that are commonly used for the production of singing mules are the linnet and the goldfinch. Other finches, like the greenfinch and redpoll do not have much of a vocabulary so are not suitable for producing singing mules.

Roller canary

Yellow goldfinch mule cock

Goldfinches are reliable hybridisers though sexing them can be difficult. A full explanation of sexing is contained in the section on goldfinches and their hybrids (see page 38).

The other finch most popular for producing singing mules is the linnet. Linnets do not tame easily and tend to be flighty but they are normally very sociable birds and cause few problems when breeding.

Further information about breeding linnet crosses can be found in the section on linnets and their hybrids on page 92. Cock mules that do not come up to exhibition standards as type birds – and, believe me, you will breed plenty of them – can be sold as songsters, especially the pretty birds with nice white markings. These birds are ideal for the pet market although useless for the show scene.

NEW SPECIES

Another reason for breeding mules and hybrids is the possibility of producing a new species. Very occasionally a mule or hybrid is found to be fertile and so can provide the basis for a new species.

The red factor coloured canary is the bird best known for originating from a mule; a canary × red-hooded siskin. It is also said by some that the bengalese finch was also the product of a fertile hybrid as none has been recorded in the wild.

Lots of breeders in continental Europe breed mules every year in an attempt to create a new type of bird, but it must be said that, for all their efforts, new species are very, very rare.

Red-hooded siskin *Carduelis cucullata*

Red factor canary from a hybrid

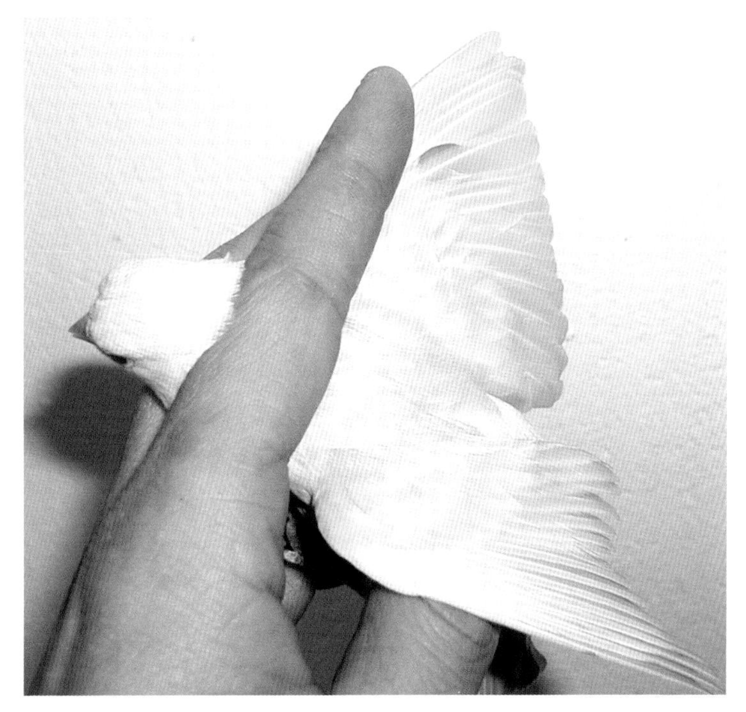

Satinette greenfinch hen

Peathroat and cheveral goldfinch

CLEAR MULES

In my eyes all mules – that is to say crosses between British finches and canaries – have their own distinctive individual beauty. However, it cannot be denied that some do better than others when put on the show bench; because of both their rarity and their beauty.

Clear mules are birds with no dark feathers at all and if I had to select one type of mule to breed, to create the most interest among those who saw it and to be certain of winning on the show bench, it would have to be a clear linnet or a clear goldfinch mule. Even then, it would need to display good size so its canary parent would have to be a Norwich.

No pairings absolutely guarantee the production of clear mules, so over the years various theories have been put forward for increasing the possibilities. Some people believe that the production of clear goldfinch mules is made more likely if the peathroat or cheveral goldfinch is used.

This theory, interesting though it is, has never been proved. A peathroat goldfinch has a spot in its blaze and white shows through. A cheveral's split is longer covering the entire lower half of the blaze which may be a thin line or a very broad line. Birds similar in appearance to true, clear mules can be produced from some coloured canaries but these are, in effect, just colour variants and do not come into the same category as clear mules for rarity or desirability.

Colour variant mules that have been bred from the lutino and satinette greenfinches are sometimes seen on the show bench. Although these birds give the appearance of being clear, the lutino cross has red eyes whereas a true clear mule has dark eyes. The satinette cross has brown stripes down its back and a dark underdown which can be seen when the bird is held in the hand and its feathers blown away from its body. Again, these are not clear mules which not only have dark eyes but also have light underdown. Top quality clear mules are so rare that they are remembered for many years after they were seen on the show bench.

The choice of canary, when trying to breed clear mules has always been deemed important. Many of our predecessors in the fancy, some of whom were experts at muling, claimed that the odds of producing clear mules were increased by breeding sibling, cinnamon canaries (sib-bred). The cinnamons were the palest obtainable and they were paired together year after year. The variegation became paler and paler with successive generations, until none of the youngsters being bred showed any marks at all. However, a feature of cinnamons is that they have pink eyes and no matter how clear the plumage of the youngsters, they were still identifiable as cinnamons. The advocates of this approach claimed that pairing these clear, cinnamon canaries with British finches increased the chances of breeding clear mules. I have no evidence to prove this and I doubt it ever was the case, although I do know that some of our forefathers swore by it.

The most famous specimen of a clear mule was a very rare, nearly clear linnet mule exhibited by Messrs Duncan and Logan at the 1911 Crystal Palace show. According to a show report of the day, this bird created quite a stir. Drawings and paintings of this mule were produced to record what the bird looked like; because, of course, photographs

Duncan and Logan's celebrated clear linnet mule winner at 1911 Crystal Palace show

of birds were rare in those days.

Another famous mule, and almost as rare as the linnet mule, was the lightly marked, siskin mule bred by Oswin Smith of Defford, in Worcestershire. This bird won Best Hybrid at the 1955 National and the Supreme Award at the January 1959 National Exhibition for its then owner, Mr. J. E. Williams. I specify January as there were two National Exhibitions in 1959; one in January and one in December. At the 1964 Scottish National, J. R. Ferguson exhibited a variegated siskin mule.

No matter how rare and interesting a variety of clear mule might be it is always the clear goldfinch mule that attracts the most interest. In 1959 the runner up at the Scottish National was an evenly marked, yellow goldfinch mule exhibited by J. Wardrop. At the 1961 Hounslow show, J. J. White won with a two-pointed, otherwise clear, goldfinch mule. It was reported that there were seven canary × bullfinch hybrids in one class at that same event.

The 1982 National saw a light goldfinch mule take the top award, the Haddon Trophy, for the Oldknow and Brankin partnership. Another famous, light goldfinch mule took the National Supreme Award on two occasions for Walter Jones of North Wales. There are many who believe that this was the best example of a clear goldfinch mule that has ever been seen on the show bench.

A noted, unevenly marked goldfinch mule exhibited by Mr F. Archer, 1911 winner at Crystal Palace and second at the Scottish National

At the National Exhibition at Olympia in 1963, R.E. Pearce won Best Mule or Hybrid with a near clear greenfinch mule. In 1968, a lightly marked, buff greenfinch mule won the Supreme Award for the Sharland and Nicholls partnership. This bird also won Best Mule or Hybrid at the 1970 Scottish National.

Lightly marked, buff greenfinch mule
Large, yellow specimens of clear mules are difficult to produce and are rarely seen.

FOSTERING

The final, and most popular reason, for keeping canaries in a British bird room, even one that is breeding mules and hybrids, is to help rear some species.

Some mules are difficult to rear. The hens lay but do not incubate their eggs. Some sit too tightly and others will not feed their chicks when they hatch. Smaller types of canary are very good feeders and make perfect foster parents for difficult pairs. All mule breeders should keep a few pairs of canaries as insurance. They just might save your best mule.

Be careful though because they may also just let it die. There are never any guarantees with hybridising. If I am lucky enough to hatch three or four young and I can't trust the parents, I will sometimes split the nest between three or four foster pairs. Usually however, just one mule or hybrid hatches, especially when the species is rare. Another reason to use foster parents is that the breeding pair will go to nest three or four times if they don't have to rear young, so the potential to breed more young is increased. I remember once having five rounds from a twite cock with a canary. I bred 13 young from that pair in one season. The same year, I also bred five from another pair. It was so nice to have 18 mules to choose from. That said however, out of 18 birds only seven were cocks, and of those only three were yellows. It is never easy. Keeping canaries also helps in those bad years when all your muling attempts fail; at least you should have been able to breed a few canaries to soften the blow. Quality canaries are not necessary for fostering. Indeed, mongrel canaries seem to be better feeders than show quality stock.

Young yellow buntings

Canary × bullfinch hybrid

CANARY AND FINCH CROSSES

Canary × bullfinch

The canary bullfinch cross is the most brightly coloured of the canary crosses, especially when its canary parent is a yellow-feathered Norwich. It does very well on the show bench, particularly when colour fed. Like all the bullfinch crosses, it is a very difficult bird to breed, but well worth the effort. Bullfinch hens are used in this cross, as the bullfinch cock has never crossed successfully with any other species. This hybrid is very rare but throughout the mid 1970s and 80s we saw an upsurge in the number bred. Even during the 1950s and 60s there always seemed to be a canary bullfinch cross on the winners list at major events.

I remember in the 1970s seeing seven canary bullies at one show. Ron Phillips reports in his book, *The History of the Scottish British Bird and Mule Club*, that in 1961 there were seven in one class at Hounslow. We saw some excellent quality birds then but, because of the intense competition, they never won. Had these birds been bred at any other time, they would have been Best in Show winners. Probably the best bird I saw during this time was bred by George Rodgers of Cannock. He bred three in 1978. Two of them were exceptional and won many prizes.

Two other good canary bullfinch crosses of that time were bred by Colin Clarke and Ray Fletton. Colin's won the Supreme Award at the English National in 1974 while Ray's did the same in 1977. John Broadbent also won in 1979 with the same Ray Fletton bird. Other canary bullfinch crosses of note were bred by Dave Williams, Tony Buck-

The late Grosvenor Ridgway, who won the Supreme Award twice with a yellow bunting in 2000 and with a greenfinch in 1985

ley and Walter Jones. Probably the best canary bullfinch hen hybrid I ever saw was exhibited by Grosvenor Ridgway.

The best, coloured specimen I have seen belonged to Terry Roberts. Over the years, Terry Roberts has shown many wonderful hybrids, but it is the coloured one that won the Best Mule or Hybrid award at the 1985 National Exhibition, which I remember most clearly.

Canary × goldfinch

The canary goldfinch cross must be the most popular of the many mules bred each year, but it is seldom bred with a canary cock and a goldfinch hen. It is much easier to use a goldfinch cock with a canary hen. Always use heavily variegated or self canary cocks, if possible. Clear cocks produce the odd light feather and split blazes in the young, which spoil the birds for the show bench because light feathers are classed as a fault. Even when using self birds, this cross nearly always produces birds with odd light feathers or a split blaze under the beak. Yellow mules show excellent dark, rich, coloration and show good definition, whereas buff birds tend to lack this richness and definition.

Buffs also show a greyish tinge around the blaze. Buff mules do not react to colour feeding quite as well. The edges of the buff feathers have a silver tinge giving a frosted appearance, whereas the yellow takes the colour right to the end of the feather, so giving a deeper colour with a more even balance. The buff feather tends to be longer than the yellow, making buffs seem larger. The feathers of buffs are not as tight and compact as those of yellows, so yellows are generally superior in every way with the exception of size. When judging dark goldfinch mules, the bird must be rich and dark with well defined markings. The feather texture should be like silk. Size is important but not to the detriment of colour. The bird should be well balanced.

Many unusual and interestingly coloured goldfinch mules are now being produced as a result of the variety of goldfinch cock colours. However, a good, dark yellow goldfinch mule cock will still win on the show bench. As with linnet mules, this bird is an exceptional songster, but it is more sought after than the linnet mule because of its colour. It is pretty to look at as well as a fantastic singer, especially

Immature canary × bullfinch
Bred by John Morris in 2006.

Francis Brankin (centre) and the late Derek Oldknow (right) being presented with the Haddon Trophy by John Haith in 1982

when trained to sing pure finch song.

The clear goldfinch mule is very rare. The clear body, reddish head and yellow suffusion of the wings make it a most striking hybrid. Again, the yellow version is the one to aim for. There are a few small, clear mules bred each year, but the large, clear yellow is nearly as rare as the clear linnet and siskin mule. Occasionally, a large, clear yellow mule does crop up. In 1982, a light goldfinch mule, owned by Oldknow and Brankin, took the National Exhibition Supreme Award.

Another famous light goldfinch mule was owned by Walter Jones from North Wales. This bird won the Supreme Award in 1991 and 1992. Many observers, including myself, believe that this was the best example of a clear goldfinch mule that has ever been seen on the show bench. Goldfinch mules have won the Supreme Award seven times in the National Exhibition's 60 year history. In fact, mules and hybrids have won this award 16 times in those 60 years.

Canary × crossbill

The canary crossbill cross is a good-sized and pleasingly colourful mule. The mule hens show distinct pencilling on their chests while the cocks' chests are clear. This cross is much more likely to be successful if a cock canary is paired with a hen crossbill. Canary × crossbill mules are now bred in a variety of colours including cinnamon and satinette.

Without doubt, the Norwich canary is the best mate for a crossbill. If the intention is to produce a crossbill × canary, using the Norwich canary helps. Its larger size is more compatible with the crossbill than the smaller canary types. As well as size, the Norwich also gives the mule the correct shape for the show bench. Small, snaky, sinewy mules of any breed never make winners. Large, cobby, yellow mules with good colour are the ones to breed. Yellow crossbill mule cocks should be a very deep red in colour, almost the same colour as a red factor canary.

In 1964, J. Dalrymple of Annan in Scotland benched a crossbill × canary cock to take the Supreme Award at the National Exhibition at Olympia. He returned a year later and repeated his win with the same bird. According to crossbill expert Ron Phillips, in his *History of the Scottish British Bird and Mule Club*, top British bird expert, Walter Lewis, declared: 'It is the most wonderful hybrid I have ever seen.' Ron Phillips also bred a quality example of this cross in 2002.

Ron Phillips' canary × crossbill hen

These crosses, however, are certainly not as rare today as they once were. Since this cross was achieved for the first time, we have seen quite a few examples. Some have certainly been superior to J. Dalrymple's which is not to detract from his great achievement of being the first to do it. I am sure that in the future, with more frequent breeding, we will see even better examples. More recently we have begun to see new crosses and colour variant cross-bill hybrids.

Don Footitt has also succeeded in breeding a superb example of this hybrid using a Norwich canary cock paired to a crossbill hen. This year, 2006, he is exhibiting probably the best buff bird I have seen. Unflighted, it is a giant of a bird with an excellent colour for its size, particularly for a buff. It was probably bred from the larger parrot crossbill.

Linnet × canary

A good, steady, dark yellow canary linnet cross mule takes some beating on the show bench. This cross should be large, with a rich and dark colour, showing no light feathers, good pencilling and rich, red coloration extending well down the chest and on the crown. Colour feeding all dark birds is essential. Occasionally, colour variant hens, mainly cinnamon, are exhibited although these are rare birds. I remember Terry Ball showing a cinnamon hen in the early 1990s. He also had cinnamon linnets at that time.

From time to time, the odd pied linnet comes along but there are only a few light feathers on these birds. A very close friend of mine, Jeff Hulme, has been breeding pied linnets for a few years now. He has not yet produced a 50 per cent light bird, but he regularly breeds birds with a few light feathers. Hopefully, in the next few years, he will be the first to breed the clear mule.

Breeding a clear linnet mule would be the ultimate achievement, bringing the breeder lasting fame, especially if the mule was a yellow cock. Even a bird carrying technical marks should do the same, especially if the markings were evenly displayed. I cannot recall ever seeing a bird like this in 35 years of attending shows. According to our early records, though, a few were shown before 1910. There were a couple of four pointers and several two pointers, either both eye marked or wing marked. Most of the variegated birds that were bred were buffs. Only a few were yellows.

In 1911 at the Crystal Palace Show, Messrs Duncan and Logan exhibited the clear, yellow linnet mule I have already described (pages 18–19).

Linnet mules are probably our best songsters, especially when they sing pure finch song. This can be achieved by moving young birds from their parents into another shed or room where they cannot hear canaries. They should be kept with a cock linnet and a training tape should be played to them for a few hours each day until the end of the first moult.

Canary × greenfinch

It is easier to breed mules from a canary greenfinch cross, if the cock is the canary and the hen is the greenfinch. This is because the cock greenfinch is less willing to hybridise than most other types of finch. Hybrid young produced from a greenfinch cock never seem to be as good as birds bred the other way round, as these hybrids take their size and shape more from the Norwich canary than the greenfinch.

Young greenfinch mules

Canary × greenfinches can be bred in a wide range of colour forms, because of the high number of colour varieties of greenfinches (cinnamon, lutino, silver and satinette). They also breed very well in cages, but have no song of any note. This bird should be the same shape as the cobby greenfinch, but slightly longer and much larger. Again yellow cocks tend to do best on the show bench. Occasionally, a good, close-feathered, well-coloured buff is bred and these birds are also worth exhibiting. Again dark mules of this variety should be colour fed. Yellow hens, with good flank pencilling, are very attractive show birds, but buff hens are of no use on the show bench.

The clear greenfinch mule is the most sought after variety of this hybrid and is very rare. Only a few of these birds have ever been bred. Over the last 20 years a wide variety of colour variant, clear mules have appeared on the show bench, but very few dark-eyed birds. In 2005, a clear, unflighted yellow was exhibited at the Lancashire British Bird and Hybrid Club.

Baz Morris had a large yellow of good natural colour and a saddle-backed hybrid that both did well in the 1980s, if my memory serves me correctly. Baz was a consistent winner and breeder of some fine birds over the years.

The last few years have seen a large number of variegated birds, both lightly marked and pied greenfinches. Recently the best specimen for size and shape was probably a yellow, pied greenfinch of excellent size and colour bred by Jeff Hulme. It was half dark and half light. If this bird was paired to a Norwich canary, there is a great chance it would produce

The late Basil Morris

a lightly marked greenfinch mule with depth of colour, shape and size.

Pied greenfinch cock

I doubt I will ever see the perfect, clear greenfinch mule, but if I do I am sure it will have been bred from one of the pied greenfinches with white toe nails that are now bred regularly. As the years go on, these pieds will start to breed pure yellow birds just like the wild canary which also started out fully dark but, through selection, has ended up clear yellow. The greenfinch now seems to be taking the same route. Breeding a clear is like winning the lottery, but, as we have seen an upsurge in variegated greenfinch mules in the last five years, it should not be too long before one takes Best in Show. Most of the dark-eyed, light mules bred lately came from this type of greenfinch.

Some of the best, dark yellow birds have been bred by Terry McCracken, who consistently turns out good ones. There have been other good birds on the bench, but it is Terry's that come to mind. John Morris has also produced some very good, dark mules. I remember in particular his dark redpoll mule and a dark goldfinch mule. Another excellent bird of note was exhibited in 2006 by Phil Shaw and it won the All British Show.

Yellow greenfinch mule cock

Siskin × canary

The siskin canary cross is a lovely bird that is well worth breeding. When the canary is a Norwich, the resulting mules are steady and make good show birds. They are best when colour fed. Size is very important when showing this cross. Well-coloured, small birds are frequently exhibited but large, well-coloured ones are less common.

Birds that come to mind were bred by Ron Phillips, who exhibited very good siskin mules; good, dark birds showing black heads. These birds' markings were very well defined and of exceptional quality. In 1985, Ron won the award for the best unflighted mule or hybrid at the National Exhibition and in 1986 he took Best in Show at the Scottish National.

Probably the most famous, dark siskin mule was owned by Walter Lewis. This bird won seven times in succession at the National and eight times in succession at the All British.

I have never been lucky enough to see a clear or even a variegated siskin mule and look forward to doing so, but according to records Dr Galloway won Best Hybrid with one at Crystal Palace in 1909 and 1910. This bird won frequently between 1908 and 1910.

Dr Galloway's clear, yellow, siskin canary Winner of Best Hybrid at 1909 & 1910 Crystal Palace shows

The next variegated siskin mule I know of cropped up 49 years later. It won the Supreme Award at the 1959 National Exhibition of Cage and Aviary Birds (see page 29). It was bred by Oswin Smith and was exhibited by J.E. Williams. Walter Lewis wrote that this bird equalled the size of a normal dark, which rarely occurs.

Redpoll × canary

Redpoll mules are generally considered to be drab in appearance, but they are very perky and bold, taking readily to show cages. However, when colour fed, the reddish breast and head colour with their rich-chestnut back, make them very attractive. The red of the face and breast should carry right down the breast as far as possible.

Depth of colour in these mules depends on the type of canary used, with red factors being the best. Redpoll × canary mules can be bred in many colour forms because of the wide range of redpoll colours. This is a popular mule due to its pleasing nature.

Norwich canaries are necessary to breed quality exhibition birds, which makes the task more difficult because of the size difference in the birds. Using the larger, mealy redpolls makes the cross slightly easier to obtain, but generally the resulting hybrids are paler.

Redpoll × canary

Using the darker and smaller, lesser redpoll produces a much darker and well-defined specimen. Usually, yellow cocks are the best to exhibit, though I remember once when this was not the case. At the Staffordshire British Bird and Mule Club Show a few years ago, after judging the classes and sorting out most of the class winners, I was left with six birds, one of which was a buff redpoll mule. I remember thinking there must be a better yellow out of 200 mules and hybrids, but looking at the other five, I came to the conclusion that the buff mule was definitely the best of the bunch and gave it the award for best mule or hybrid.

After that show, I heard a few moans about a buff bird taking the award for best bird, but I was adamant that a good buff is better than a poor yellow, and I still hold that opinion: winners can only be chosen from the birds there on the day. A few weeks later I was glad to see the bird had won the London and Home Counties British Bird and Mule Club Show. A judge sees every bird at close quarters. Birds settle as the day goes on and can look quite different when the judge makes his or her decision compared to how they appeared at the start of the show – it is no use exhibitors judging the birds then.

The late Lyn Jones with his buff redpoll mule

I followed this bird's results closely throughout its showing life and it did better than most buffs. In 2002, the bird won Best Hybrid at the National. This mule was owned by the late Lyn Jones, who once told me that he believed that it was the best buff redpoll mule he had ever seen, and Lyn benched a lot of winners in his time.

Twite × canary

Another buff bird that did well was Les Rodgers' redpoll bullfinch cross. It won the highest prize of all, the Supreme Award at the National Exhibition. So don't be afraid to show quality buff birds. They can win at shows.

Twite × canary

The twite canary cross is a very attractive bird, one of my favourites in fact. It can be seen at its best when it has been colour fed and the canary is a Norwich. A twite mule resembles a smaller linnet mule but the body is much darker and the beak paler and more slender. They have smaller heads, heavier pencilling and slightly longer tails, and make good show birds.

Generally, this cross is reasonably easy to produce. I believe

The late John Broadbent's Best Current Year Bred goldfinch mule, Swaffam 1997

the reason we do not see more of them is because twite cocks are not so readily available as some other finches. Two great birds which I remember, were bred by Ron Phillips and Terry McCracken. Terry's won the All British in 1990. As far as I can ascertain, only one almost clear, twite mule has been bred, which was exhibited by Dr Galloway in 1909. Unlike the linnet, the twite mule has no song.

Canary × chaffinch

The canary chaffinch cross is rare, because it is difficult to breed. It would be an exceptional hybrid in its yellow form. There is only one recorded breeding in Britain, although I know of several such birds on the continent.

Goldfinch × crossbill hybrid

GOLDFINCHES AND THEIR HYBRIDS

GOLDFINCH (*CARDUELIS CARDUELIS*)

Status and distribution: A widespread and generally very common bird, breeding in the British Isles and over a large area stretching from western France and Iberia east across Europe to the Caspian Sea and Urals and north to southern parts of Norway, Sweden, Finland and Russia. In the south, it breeds on most of the larger Mediterranean islands and in Turkey, the Caucasus, the Near East, the Azores, Madeira, the Canary Isles, north-west Africa, parts of coastal Libya and in the Nile Valley. Northern and eastern populations are migratory, leaving during September and October to winter mainly within range of southern breeders and returning during March and April.

Subspecies: There are several subspecies but all are very similar. The nominate variety is found over much of Europe with slightly smaller *C. parva* in south-west Europe, north-west Africa and the Atlantic islands. The British Isles variety, *C. britannica*, which is also found in the Netherlands is slightly darker brown. The south-west Asian variety, *C. niedecki*, is paler and greyer, while the Caucasian *C. loudoni* is distinctly darker brown on top.

Habitat: These birds inhabit open woodland and forest, woodland edges and hedgerows, orchards, gardens and sometimes town parks. They are also commonly found in dry scrub, steppe and semi-desert areas.

A goldfinch clutch consists of four to six eggs, which hatch after 13 to 15 days of incubation. The young fledge at 14 days old and are self supporting at 28 days.

Sexing goldfinches

Sexing goldfinches can be difficult, but there are a number of indicators. The blaze above the cock's eye comes past the eye, while on the hen it cuts back behind the eye. The cock's shoulder butts and head are solid black, unlike the hen's which have a brown suffusion to them. When in breeding condition, the black stripe down the beaks of both cock and hen disappears and their beaks become pure white. When the goldfinch cock is in peak condition he will swirl his body from left to right, swinging his tail with short bursts of song, as if he is doing the twist, the popular dance from the 1960s. This is called 'proud tailing' and is always a sign of good condition.

When bred in cages, some goldfinch cocks can damage the eggs so, because eggs are laid early in the morning, the cock should be removed at night and not returned until the egg has been removed and replaced with a dummy egg. The riskier alternative is to be sure to be awake early enough to remove the egg as it is laid. Both sexes of the young hybrids look identical until after the moult when the blaze becomes visible. It is customary to colour feed goldfinch mules.

Goldfinch × greenfinch

The goldfinch greenfinch cross is a lovely hybrid, which does very well on the show bench. It shows its parentage on both sides well, but has a neck fault which is commonly seen with goldfinch crosses (see page 52). This is the best way round to breed this hybrid. It is probably the easiest hybrid to try and a very good pairing with which to start.

Goldfinch × linnet

While no hybrid is easy to produce, another hybrid that is easier to breed than most is the goldfinch linnet cross. This hybrid has the appearance of a good-coloured linnet with a red blaze and yellow wing bars. A full blaze on this cross is rare. It tends to be very snaky in the head, normally full on the forehead only and shows both parents well. No red

Goldfinch cock

Goldfinches are very reliable hybridisers.

cap is visible on the hens, and they are duller generally in body colour. This cross is not often seen on the show bench, but it has a very lively disposition and the cock's song is excellent, very sharp, the notes being short but musical.

Goldfinch × siskin

The goldfinch siskin cross is a very lively hybrid. The mating is helped because the goldfinch and siskin are closely related. It is not as colourful as one would expect, but very friendly and relatively easy to breed.

Breeding the cross using a goldfinch hen seems to improve the definition and depth of colour slightly. Both parents can be clearly seen in this hybrid, which has a blend of subtle colours.

I do not think I have ever seen one of these birds take Best in Show at a major event, but they settle in a show cage well. This cross looks like a large siskin but is more brilliantly coloured. It also carries the dark cap of the siskin with just a flush of the goldfinch's blaze, giving a very pretty effect.

The goldfinch siskin cross is a small hybrid unless the northern goldfinch is used. The hen of this cross is again rather dull, lacking the cock's rich, yellow tone of body colour and blaze.

Goldfinch × redpoll

The goldfinch redpoll cross, like the siskin × goldfinch, is popular, relatively easy to produce and well worth trying. It has rich coloration and is a very steady bird, making it an ideal show specimen. Its bright colours beautifully complement the habits of the redpoll. A good specimen should be dark chestnut with good flank markings and red coloration extending well down the chest. For the best results, this hybrid should be colour fed.

The mealy redpoll produces a larger but paler hybrid, so for good colour it is better to use a good, lesser redpoll.

Goldfinch × chaffinch

I believe the first recorded cross from a goldfinch chaffinch pairing was achieved in 1958 by Mr R. Tout – it was possibly this that was shown at the Scottish National in 1963 by J. E. Williams. However, in *Mules and Hybrid Birds*, Victor Carr claims that his father, Percy, was the first to produce one in 1959. Certainly, it was not until much later that the next of example to be bred was shown at the Yorkshire British Bird and Hybrid Club Show in 1991, though it was very disappointing.

This is a very difficult cross to produce and only a few have ever been bred. Although it shows the characteristics of both parents well, this cross is unfortunately quite drab. The white wing bars of the chaffinch show a yellowish tinge, while the head and beak are typical of chaffinch hybrids.

As chaffinch cocks and both male and female goldfinches are so colourful, the hybrid might be expected to be very bright. Unfortunately, as with all chaffinch hybrids, the chaffinch colours are never passed on, just some of its markings and its shape. If we could breed hybrids from the chaffinch cock, they might be more colourful, but none has been bred yet. Both the hybrids bred to date were hens, and it is thought when a cock is produced it will look different. Only time will tell.

Fledgling goldfinch × redpoll

GOLDFINCH × BRAMBLEFINCH

According to Victor Carr, this hybrid has been claimed once, but I have no other record of this cross.

GOLDFINCH × TWITE

A goldfinch twite cross has been produced on two occasions as far as I am aware. According to Peter Degville, Sid Humphries bred and exhibited one, though I am unsure whether a goldfinch or twite cock was used. Neither method should present any problem.

The second person I know to bred this hybrid was Willie Walsh, who bred three in 1995 using a goldfinch cock. One of these hybrids won the award for Best Current Year Bred at the Southern Native Show in Ireland. Why this cross is not seen more often is a mystery. The only reason I can think of is that few are attempting it. The twite is also called the mountain linnet and is closely related to the linnet and the redpoll. As both these species cross well, they would be worth a try.

GOLDFINCH × CROSSBILL

The first goldfinch crossbill hybrid I am aware of was exhibited at Pescara in Italy in 1999. The cross showed both parents well but would have been richer in colour if colour fed. Another example was shown at the 2002 World Show in Belgium. I believe it had been bred the other way round, using a crossbill cock.

Due to the size difference, it would seem impossible to breed this way round with the English goldfinch. It would be hard to achieve even with the larger Siberian goldfinch. The bird shown in Belgium had the coloration of a goldfinch mule with the shape, beak, rump colour and wings of the crossbill. It was not as thickset as the crossbill but showed both parents

The late Peter Bailey
at the Scottish
British Bird & Mule Club

equally. While putting the finishing touches to this book, I heard that Don Footit had just bred three of these hybrids in one nest and that the pair was still nesting. This being the case, it is the first time this cross has been bred in the UK. At this point, I am unaware whether these birds were bred from an English or a northern goldfinch.

The late Peter Lander

Peter Lander was a founder member of the British Bird Breeders' Association, founder of the British Bird Council and instrumental in preparing information for ring sizes ahead of the Countryside and Wildlife Act 1981.

Goldfinch × crossbill

BULLFINCHES AND THEIR HYBRIDS

Common (northern) bullfinch (*Pyrrhula pyrrhula*)

Status and distribution: Widely distributed and common. Breeds throughout the British Isles and France, from northern Spain east across Europe to the Urals including much of Scandinavia except the far north and higher mountains and as far north as the White Sea in Russia. In the south, breeding areas extend to the Mediterranean coast of France, northern Italy and the Balkans, northern Turkey and the Caucasus.

Migratory in the far north of the range, partial migrant or resident elsewhere. Migrants move southwards in October and November, returning in March and April. More widespread in winter, especially in Iberia, south and south-east Europe and Turkey. Vagrants recorded in Iceland, Gibraltar, north-west Africa, Sicily, Malta and Jordan.

Subspecies: Several subspecies occur, differing in intensity of colour in the male and very slightly in overall size. Nominate race is largest and occurs in northern parts of Scandinavia and Russia, with the very similar *P. europoea* ranging from the Pyrenees to Germany. The slightly smaller *P. pileata*, the male of which is darker grey above and duller pink below, occurs in the British Isles. Compared to the nominate, the *P. iberiae* male from northern Iberia is more orange below with some red on the back, while females are paler above. *P. rossikowi* from northern Turkey and the Caucasus is deeper, more reddish-pink below.

Habitat: Woodland and open forest, usually deciduous

but also coniferous in the north. Also found on farmland with copses and hedgerows, orchards, gardens and town parks. A generally shy and secretive bird.

Eggs hatch 11 days after sitting begins. Young leave the nest at about 13 days and are self-supporting at approximately 28 days old.

The popularity of the bullfinch, both as a British bird in its own right and for hybridising, is matched only by that of the goldfinch. The reason is not difficult to see as these two birds are very colourful, and they produce excellent mules and hybrids. Some mule and hybrid breeders have claimed that they have crossed cock bullfinches with other species, but this has never been proved. This does not mean that it will never be done. Indeed, you might be the first one to do it.

A more conventional approach to breeding bullfinch hybrids, however, requires only hen bullfinches. It is still an

Bullfinch hen

enormous challenge, but it is worth it because the bullfinch range of hybrids is not only colourful but also powerful, and that is what makes them such popular winners.

Select dark, rich, yellow-feathered bullfinch hens because paler birds rarely breed good hybrids. Bullfinch hens are so sought after that you may not be able to pick and choose, but make every effort to obtain only the best and deepest-coloured birds. I wish I had a pound for every time the phone has rung and a caller has asked, 'Do you have any spare bullfinches or goldfinches?'

Bullfinch hybrids can be bred in both large cages and aviaries. Hybridising pairs need to be kept separate from others, so aviaries measuring six feet high by two feet wide and six feet deep are the most suitable.

I prefer an aviary with a solid clear roof, solid back and sides, a mesh front and a mesh-covered walkway in front of that to give the pair protection and security from outside interference. Covering the whole roof with perspex stops bad weather from damaging the nest. Some British birds build their nests in the daftest of places, so cold weather, rain, cats or hawks might disturb the nest if the roof is not covered.

I put my hybridising pairs together before Christmas to create a pair bond. I then split the pairs for two weeks around mid-April, prior to breeding. Putting the birds together in the winter also helps to avoid some aggression when they are put back together and are in breeding condition.

As with most hybrid pairs, bullfinch hens produce a large number of clear eggs. In fact, bullfinch hens are masters (or mistresses) at it. Hybrid breeding is difficult. Rarely do you get full clutches and pairs regularly only chip out one youngster. This makes the task more difficult, because hens get bored with only one youngster to rear and are liable to let them die. In cases like this, canaries or greenfinches make excellent foster parents for bullfinch hybrids. And not having to feed chicks encourages the hybrid pair to go to nest again more quickly.

June to August is the best time to breed hybrids, but I have bred them in May and September. Rearing birds in September, though, can be difficult. With the onset of the main moult, most of your feeder pairs will not be available. So be prepared to hand feed late-bred youngsters or at least top up the young yourself early in the morning, a few times through the day and at dusk.

Most hybrid eggs hatch at 12 days. Young usually leave the nest at 14 days old, but should be left with their parents until they are eating well on their own. But don't leave the young with the parents for longer than is necessary. As soon as they are eating, move them. They will come on much more quickly once they are feeding themselves adequately. This is normally between 24 and 28 days old.

If you are ever lucky enough to have several fertile bullfinch eggs from any bullfinch hen, try not to foster the young too early. Of course, if circumstances demand it then you must but, generally, finch hens are better feeders than most canaries and your best chance of rearing is by leaving well alone, especially with bullfinch hybrids. I believe that these hybrids do better when left with their parents, especially for the first week.

Some canaries will refuse to rear bullfinch hybrids from the egg. I believe that bullfinch chicks' heads wave around when very young and canaries do not devote enough time to making sure each one is fed, instead feeding the bird with the largest mouth and the ones which keep their heads still. A further point is that bullfinch hybrids need more protein than canaries in the first week and the bullfinch hen will supply livefood. You can, of course, add this to the canaries' softfood if required. This is where experienced bird keepers score over the novice. They watch their birds and experience allows them to make the right decisions about feeding and fostering. Making the wrong decision can be heartbreaking.

The Northern Debate

Size used to be the main criterion when breeding hybrids, but nowadays colour and definition are generally accepted as being more important. Size is only relevant to the particular finches used with the cross. These days, northern and Siberian hybrids are frowned upon on the English show bench, unless they are shown in classes specifically for northern birds. Years ago Siberian bullfinches and goldfinches were used regularly for hybridising but, today, judges have to be careful. In some shows a hybrid carrying northern blood may take a prize in the main classification. In others, however, if there is a class for northern mules and hybrids, then that's the class they should be in.

The show standard for British bird hybrids still says 'as large as possible', but this can be interpreted in two ways. What it actually means is 'as large as possible taking into account that it has been bred from a British bird'. It must never be forgotten that we are talking about the British bird section and the birds in it should be British birds or bred from British birds. Northern birds therefore, should be exhibited in the classes put on for them, and if there are no classes then they should not be at the show.

There is, of course, a contradiction to this. At least six varieties of the mealy redpoll are distributed across Europe; some small, some large, some pale and some dark. Using any of the redpoll varieties is acceptable, but hybrids bred from the larger redpolls, although bigger, always seem less rich in colour than those bred from the darker, lesser redpoll. In my opinion, it is far more important to produce a colourful hybrid than a massive hybrid, but one that combines both colour and size is the Best in Show winner every time.

As size is relevant to the species used, you would not expect to see a goldfinch bullfinch cross bred from the English goldfinch and bullfinch to be as large as one bred from the northern goldfinch and northern bullfinch. To safeguard the keeping of the British goldfinch and bullfinch, we cannot judge based on size alone. Otherwise, we will stop keeping the smaller varieties of goldfinch and bullfinch. Having said that, the smaller English species do produce darker, well-coloured hybrids, with better definition than the northern and European alternatives. Even birds like goldfinch mules are larger when crossed with European goldfinches but they lack depth of colour and definition. A good judge will see this and should not give preference to size alone.

For some reason goldfinch crosses seem to be accepted, as are the larger, northern ranges of goldfinch. It seems to be the bullfinch where most of the trouble occurs. This is probably because hybrids from the bullfinch are rare and probably win more Best in Shows than any other hybrid. It is a fact that bullfinch hybrids bred from the northern varieties are much more prolific and easier to breed than the English bullfinch, so English birds should score on the grounds of rarity. I have heard of three or four greenfinch bullfinch crosses being bred in one nest from northern birds.

This rarely happens when English birds are used. Then

usually only one egg, or occasionally two, are fertile and it is unusual to be able to rear the bird successfully. We are lucky in Britain if we see one or two bred each year. Exhibitors will always try to sneak the larger northern hybrids into the British classes until we allow best northern bird to go for Best in Show. If we allowed that, we would soon see the northern hybrids in their own classes, where the competition is less intense.

I believe we should cater for the northern species. They are wonderful birds in their own right. However, this should not be to the detriment of our own English species. There is room in our shows for both, but all clubs should have the same criteria. Exhibitors should be honest about the way their birds are bred and, if judges were more critical and did not judge on size alone, we could allow northern hybrids to go for Best in Show.

We could have special categories for best British bird hybrid and for best northern bird hybrid. Which one took the award for best in show would not matter. Such action would prevent northern birds being the main subject of conversation at shows. It would also aid judges and help stop animosity towards them when they class birds wrongly or, as some do, push the northern birds back in the class to avoid controversial decisions.

Creating different categories for British and northern birds might also help to boost the numbers of birds exhibited at our shows and stop the decline. Any action we can take to increase entries and visitors to our events must be good for the hobby.

Goldfinch × bullfinch

The goldfinch bullfinch cross is probably the easiest bullfinch cross to produce with the possible exception of the linnet × bullfinch. It is very colourful and a good bird for the show bench.

The fertility of this hybrid seems higher than others, as nests of two, three and occasionally four are reared. Bullfinch hens do make good rearers as long as they have three or four young to feed.

Problems associated with goldfinch × bullfinch hybrids are an undesirable parting of the neck feathers, too much black mask around the face and a line running under the beak down the chest, as though the feathers had a parting. This line makes the bird look as though it has been rubbing against the cage bars. Many goldfinch hybrids also suffer from this fault, especially the goldfinch greenfinch cross.

The goldfinch bullfinch hybrid's crimson blaze should run well down to the breast, the further the better, and it should be similar in size to a good English bullfinch.

The bird's habits resemble the bullfinch with its pleasing and steady nature and it should show none of the restlessness of the goldfinch. Its song is low, very sweet and continuous.

Linnet × bullfinch

Along with the goldfinch bullfinch cross, the linnet bullfinch hybrid is probably the easiest bullfinch hybrid to produce.

The rich vermilion tint of the breast, throat, cheeks and forehead is marvellous, while the back colour is the rich brown of the linnet, though without the stripes or spangles. Some of these birds, however, lack the red or orange tint associated with the cross, and some are too dark. Buff examples, as with most hybrids, do not compare well with their yellow counterparts. The hen, like the bullfinch hen, lacks the breast colour of the cock and is much more sombre in colour.

This hybrid does not steady down easily. It is far more restless than the goldfinch bullfinch cross, a trait inherited from the linnet. The cocks are excellent songsters, another trait from the linnet, and their shape, like their colour, is a perfect blend of both parents.

Canary × bullfinch

The canary bullfinch cross seems to have the longest lifespan of all the bullfinch hybrids. These birds show a distinct pencilling on a slate-coloured back and, when colour fed, make a super hybrid capable of winning at most major shows. This is especially true when the hybrid is bred from a Norwich canary. A yellow-feathered specimen has less pronounced pencilling than a buff.

The hen canary bullfinch hybrid is the most colourful female of this group of hybrids. They are actually mules but, in most major shows, they are included in the hybrid section rather than the mule section – perhaps in recognition of the difficulty of producing them.

During the 1980s, we saw quite a few good specimens of this hybrid, with this cross dominating the shows over a 10 year period. To have so many quality hybrids bred in such a short period of time was astounding.

In my opinion, the two best were exhibited by George Rogers. Other notable examples I can remember were a really colourful hybrid exhibited by Terry Roberts, another benched by G. Upex and one shown by C. Clarke.

Greenfinch × bullfinch

It could be argued that the greenfinch × bullfinch should be one of the easiest bullfinch hybrids to breed, as the greenfinch is so domesticated. In fact, it is one of the hardest hybrids to breed, even more difficult than the canary × bullfinch. I believe the reason it is so difficult is because of the low fertility of greenfinch cocks. Most hybrid pairs containing a greenfinch cock produce far fewer young than pairs involving a greenfinch hen. However, as we have already seen, a greenfinch hen is not an option when trying to breed crosses from bullfinches and greenfinches.

Chaffinch cocks also have comparatively low fertility. Perhaps the sperm from these cocks is not very strong. Yet goldfinch, linnet and redpoll cocks do not seem to have any fertility problems. The low fertility of greenfinch and chaffinch cocks is possibly due to the sperm just not being as compatible with the hens of other finch varieties.

However, although difficult to breed as a result, the greenfinch × bullfinch is a wonderful cross. A yellow cock has everything required of a hybrid. Colour feeding is essential to bring out the depth of colour and, if a reasonable specimen is produced, it is a potential Best in Show winner.

This cross is very similar in appearance to the canary × bullfinch with a slate-grey back without distinct pencilling but with a slight tinge of the greenfinch's green. There is a display of rich, reddish orange on the breast, throat and cheeks. The rump should be the same colour, while the head should be dark. The wings are a curious mixture of both parents – barred like the bullfinch, but slightly tinted with reddish orange. The main flight feathers are tinted with the greenfinch's yellow, and the tail is dark. Colour fed, this hybrid is richer and darker than the canary bullfinch cross. The hen is darker and duller, lacking the reddish orange of the cock. Like all bullfinch hybrids, a varied range of colour forms of this bird has been achieved. However, I would use only normal greenfinch cocks, as this helps to keep the hybrids darker and better defined.

Linnet × bullfinch family

Crossbill × bullfinch

Though difficult to breed, examples of the crossbill bullfinch hybrid are beginning to appear on the show bench. Along with the redpoll × bullfinch, this bird used to be very rare, but many more crossbills are now being kept and bred and some of these are being used to produce hybrids. So we should see even more of them in the future.

The first-ever hybrid from this cross was shown at the Yorkshire British Bird and Mule Club Show in 2002, by Wendy Woodward. It was the first time it had ever been seen on the show bench in Britain, although this bird was bred from a northern bullfinch. A hen was shown at the Staffordshire British Bird and Mule Club Show in 2003, by G. Cheeseman. It was an unflighted, buff hen bred in the UK by Dale Bowen. Dale also bred a cock, but this bird died before it had fully moulted. Another crossbill × bullfinch cock was reared in 2005, bred by Mike Holland. Unfortunately, this bird died before it reached the show bench, although it did reach adult plumage. These were the first crossbill bullfinch cross cocks to be bred in the UK. In 1981, *Cage and Aviary Birds* reported that a crossbill × bullfinch had been bred in West Germany.

Redpoll × bullfinch

Both the redpoll and the bullfinch tend to be ready breeders so the redpoll bullfinch cross should be easy to breed, but it isn't. It is one of the most difficult, and the hybrids they produce rarely live longer than two to three years. This cross is the smallest of the bullfinch hybrids, and although it is acceptable to use any of the European redpolls, the lesser redpoll and the English bullfinch are best because this combination produces the best depth of colour. Some breeders believe that the lesser redpoll is too

Crossbill × bullfinch

small to breed with the much larger bullfinch, preferring the mealy redpoll as the easier option. This may be the case, but in the last 10 years we have seen hybrids bred from lesser redpolls on a few occasions. The best example of this cross I have ever seen was bred by Mick Booth of Cheshire. At its best, this hybrid was unbeatable. It was a yellow and very rich in colour. I am sure that had this bird been exhibited at the National Exhibition, it would have taken the Supreme Award.

Redpoll × bullfinch
bred by Mick Booth

Larret Franks (left) and the author at Yorkshire BB & HC show 2002

Three redpoll bullfinch crosses have won the Supreme Award at the National. The first, shown by the Lloyd and Story partnership, took the award at the 1951 National, the first National to feature the Haddon Trophy. The second was a buff, bred by Les Rodgers, and the third was owned by Walter Jones, who has taken the Haddon Trophy on three occasions.

Making sure you have a redpoll cock can be difficult. One way to be certain in a youngster not being colour fed is to pluck a few feathers from its chest and put the bird on colour food for a few weeks. If the plucked area turns red you can be sure it is a cock bird. Redpolls are very friendly. They are also great parents and will make a fuss of any bird that is willing to be fussed over. Perhaps it is only their size that stops lots of this hybrid being bred.

This hybrid resembles the linnet bullfinch cross in colour with a rich vermilion breast and cheeks and a dark head and bib. The back resembles that of the redpoll and the hybrid's size is between that of its bullfinch and redpoll parents. The head is quite small with the body shape resembling a cobby redpoll. The flight feathers of the wings are dark with a bar of light brown across them. It is a very cheerful and lively bird with many of the redpoll's habits, but it has no song of any note. After the three specimens I have described, no redpoll bullfinch hybrids were seen for many years; but during the last 20 years, there have been at least six. I remember Ron Parrish exhibiting one, and John Broadbent had another. At one show, three were exhibited in the same class, the largest class of redpoll bullfinches crosses I have seen.

Siskin × bullfinch

The siskin bullfinch hybrid has been recorded only once. I did not see the bird, but according to Victor Carr in his 1959 book *Mule and Hybrid Birds*, 'The bird was imperfect in many ways. Doubtless it was a hen bird and in consequence most uninteresting from a colour point of view.' I feel sorry for the breeder of this bird. To be the first to cross the species, find out the bird was a hen and then to see this statement in a book, with no indication of who bred it, must have been devastating. Hybrid breeding certainly isn't for the faint hearted.

Twite × bullfinch

To date, the twite bullfinch cross has never been bred and the reason for this eludes me. Both species are ready breeders. The twite is similar to the linnet and the redpoll, and the cocks of both these species have produced hybrids with bullfinch hens. Perhaps because twite cocks and bullfinch hens are difficult to get hold of, not many people have attempted this cross. So it may not be impossible. It would be great to see a twite bullfinch cross, and I am sure we will see this hybrid in the future.

Mealy redpoll

REDPOLLS AND THEIR HYBRIDS

Redpolls are very sociable and friendly. They tame very quickly and are happy to breed in either cage or aviary. There are two main types of redpoll used to produce hybrids; the lesser (*Carduelis flammea cabaret*) and the mealy (*C. f. flammea*). The mealy is larger and paler than the lesser. Mealies produce larger hybrids, but the lesser produces much richer-coloured birds.

C. f. flammea (the mealy): The mealy is characteristic of North America, Europe and Asia (holarctic) and can be found in a broad band across the Arctic, with pockets to the south in Newfoundland and central Russia. This race of redpoll is most frequently found in North America during irruptions - years in which we see major explosions of the species in a certain area then after a few years they move on.

The subspecies *C. f. holboelli* is larger and longer, with a longer bill and large bib. *C. f. rostrata*, found in Greenland, is larger and browner than *C. f. flammea*, while *C. f. icelandica*, found in Iceland, is smaller and greyer in colour.

C. f. cabaret (the lesser): Found in Europe, this is the smallest common redpoll. It is much richer in colour than the others.

C. hornemanni hornemanni (artic or hoary) is very pale in colour and is a large, light grey bird with dark, sparse pencilling, generally without streaking on the rump.

Subspecies *C. h. exilipes* is between the arctic and mealy in size and colour.

It is difficult to identify specific races of the common redpoll because of the extreme variability in each bird's plumage. It is also difficult to identify the less common hoary redpoll (*C. h. hornemanni*). Care and careful observation are a necessity.

Eggs hatch 11 days after sitting begins. Young leave the nest at about 13 days and are self-supporting at approximately 24 days old.

The English redpoll is one of the small and dark-coloured redpolls. Hybrids are also bred using the larger, paler, mealy redpoll. These birds are vagrants and winter in this country.

The only way to sex these species in confinement is to colour feed them. The cocks will then show a red chest (see page 58 for a more detailed description). Redpolls are very friendly and tame, very easy to breed and it is a delight to watch their acrobatic displays. As the redpoll has many colour forms, it is very useful for breeding various colours of mules and hybrids.

Redpoll × bullfinch

The redpoll bullfinch cross is covered under the bullfinch hybrids section of this book (see page 56). One bird not mentioned in that section was the winner of Best Hybrid and 3rd Best in Show at the National Exhibition, which was bred in July 1969 by S. Humphrey. R. Parris won Best Hybrid at the All British and Best Mule or Hybrid at the National in 1994 with another, while Walter Jones took Best Bird in Show at the Scottish National with another in 1996. At that same event, Walter took the 2nd Best in Show award with his famous light mule and 3rd Best in Show with his canary bullfinch cross, according to Ron Phillips in his book, *The History of the Scottish British Bird and Mule Club*. Also in 1996, Wendy Woodward took the award for Best Mule or Hybrid at the All British with her redpoll bullfinch cross.

Redpoll × siskin

There is very little to recommend the redpoll siskin cross. The hybrids are very drab and the only justification for breeding them that I can think of is the production of colour variant hens or to gain experience of breeding hybrids. For fuller details of this cross, see the siskin × redpoll section on page 78.

Redpoll × greenfinch

Although the redpoll greenfinch is an easy hybrid to breed, it is not popular because of its drab appearance. It looks like a large, cumbersome redpoll with a greenfinch's wings. It displays traces of the redpoll's bib, but lacks the attractive pencilling of the redpoll and the rich coloration of the greenfinch. Colour variant forms are more attractive. The redpoll greenfinch cross is worth breeding by those who are seeking to increase their experience of hybrid production, but the normal coloured bird from this mating must be colour fed to have any chance of winning on the show bench.

Redpoll × linnet

The redpoll linnet cross, being a combination of largely brown-coloured birds, is never going to rank among the most attractive of hybrids. The most attractive aspect of its appearance is the cock's breast colour when properly colour fed. The colour variant forms are more attractive, and pairings can be made with colour variant redpoll cocks in order to produce colour variant hens.

However, despite their lack of interesting colour, these hybrids are easy to breed, either way round, so can be useful for gaining experience.

Redpoll × chaffinch

The first redpoll chaffinch hybrid was bred by Percy Carr, father of the late Victor Carr. Unfortunately, the bird died before moulting into adult plumage although according to Victor, it showed every sign of being a hen. The bird was stuffed and while I did not see it myself those who did said that it looked like a chaffinch hen with a redpoll's bib. In 1963, one was shown by W. Hovelsroud at the Scottish National.

I did see the second example of this cross to be bred in 1987 by W. Gentle and was disappointed. From the colourful nature of the chaffinch cock I expected to see a colourful hybrid, but it seems that if a chaffinch is paired with any brown-hued bird the hybrids are quite drab.

It was thought that only redpoll × chaffinch hens had ever been bred because of the drabness of the hybrids and because a cock had yet to be seen. However, that does not seem to be the case. The fact is that both cock and hen from this cross are drab. Even so, I believe it is a hybrid worth breeding if only for its rarity. It has the appearance of a large redpoll with the white shoulders and beak of the chaffinch.

Redpoll × crossbill

The first time I saw a redpoll crossbill cross being exhibited in the UK was at the All British Show at Winsford in 2003. The bird, of excellent quality, colour, size and condition, was exhibited by M. Steven. It showed both its parents well and because I feel that a lesser redpoll would be too small to mate with a crossbill, I assume that a mealy redpoll was used.

A redpoll × crossbill cock, bred by Ron Phillips, won Best Current Year Bred Hybrid at the Yorkshire British Bird and Mule Club show in 2004. It was a first class, steady show bird, showing its parentage well. When colour fed it was red all through its front, from the top of its head to right down under its belly, with the flank markings of the redpoll. This lovely hybrid is well worth trying but is difficult to breed.

Redpoll × twite

The redpoll × twite resembles a redpoll linnet hybrid but has a smaller beak. Other than for breeding colour variant hens, this hybrid has little to recommend it. As it is not often bred, it could be difficult to produce and that is where any achievement may lie. Richard Lawson and his father have two or three cinnamon redpoll twite hybrids which they are attempting to cross back to the twite if one of these hybrids proves fertile. If they succeed, we may see the first cinnamon twite.

Redpoll × goldfinch

Like the siskin goldfinch cross, the redpoll goldfinch hybrid has rich, bright colours and, being steady, makes an ideal show specimen. The best examples are dark chestnut with good flank markings and the red coloration travelling well down through the chest. It is easy to breed and benefits from being colour fed. Hens show a much smaller blaze than cocks; some just show a pale hazel tint instead of a blaze. The cock has a pretty, if short, song made up of goldfinch and redpoll notes. Hybrids from the mealy redpoll are larger but paler and not as attractive as those from the lesser redpoll. This hybrid is well worth breeding.

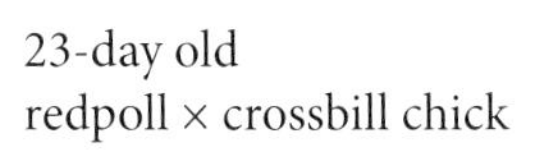

23-day old
redpoll × crossbill chick

Redpoll × bullfinch family

GREENFINCHES AND THEIR HYBRIDS

Greenfinch (*Carduelis chloris*)

Status and distribution: Widespread and abundant. Breeds in the British Isles and from western France and Iberia east through Europe to Turkey, the Caucasus and the Urals. Found north to the Arctic Circle in coastal Norway, to the head of the Gulf of Bothnia, throughout central and southern Finland and in Russia as far north as the White Sea. In the south, breeds on most larger Mediterranean islands and some of the Canaries, also in north-west Africa and the Middle East.

Northernmost populations are migratory, leaving breeding areas in September to October and returning in April. Elsewhere, a partial migrant or resident. In winter occurs more widely around the Mediterranean, particularly north Africa, on Cyprus, and in the Middle East.

Vagrants recorded on Iceland, the Faroes, in the far north of Scandinavia, on Madeira and the Canary Islands. Introduced to the Azores.

Subspecies: *C. chloris* is found over much of northern Europe but has been replaced in southern Europe and north Africa by *C. aurantiiventris* which has brighter plumage and a larger bill. However separation of greenfinch varieties in the field is difficult. *C. turkestanicus* found in the Crimean and Caucasus and *C. chlorotica* from the Near East are paler than *C. chloris* and greyer on wings and underparts.

Habitat: Open coniferous, mixed and deciduous woodland and forest edges, farmland with copses and hedgerows, large gardens and town parks. In winter, greenfinches are found often in more open habitats including stubble fields and often along coasts.

Greenfinches have become so domesticated over the last 25 years that they are now much larger and just as colourful as their wild counterpart, making them easy to use for hybridising. As a result they have been crossed with every other finch.

The greenfinch is the ideal foster parent for all hybrids and all breeders should keep a few pairs as insurance. The cock is not as prolific when hybridising as the hen. Yellows are easily distinguished from buff greenfinches and should always be used for breeding hybrids.

These birds can be affected by a parasitic infection, a symptom of which is weight loss. To combat this 'going light' as it is called these birds should be treated with Intradine or any other suitable sulpha drug prescribed by your vet as soon as the young are self-supporting. The medication should be continued until the end of the first moult. The drugs do not cure the disease but once adult, the birds' immune systems can cope with the parasite allowing them to live with it without ill effects.

I always give all my other young mules and hybrids this treatment as a precaution. I have heard it said that it is unnecessary but I don't think it's worth the risk and I have to feed it to my young greenfinches anyway.

The greenfinch has many colour variant forms such as lutino, satinette, cinnamon and silver. These can produce some very good and interesting hybrids.

Greenfinch cocks can become very aggressive when they attain breeding condition so pairings must be made after the moult in the previous year. Greenfinch cocks are not very fertile and often only produce single full eggs,

Greenfinch cock

whereas with a pairing involving a greenfinch hen there are normally three or four full eggs per clutch.

Greenfinches breed readily in cage or aviary and are available in a vast range of colours, which is why they are very popular for hybridising. The clutch is usually four to six eggs, which hatch after 13 days. Young leave the nest at about 14 to 16 days and are self supporting at approximately 28 days.

Greenfinch × goldfinch

The greenfinch goldfinch cross is easier to breed using a goldfinch cock than a greenfinch cock. This is a lovely hybrid which can do very well on the show bench. Occasionally a brilliant example is bred which takes most of the colour of the goldfinch with a large, good coloured blaze and lustrous plumage, wide wing bars of yellow and a rich green body.

Unfortunately such a colourful example is rare and the

normal bird can look a little dull. It shows the characteristics of both parents very well and is also a reasonably steady bird but regularly shows a common neck fault which is often seen with goldfinch crosses (see the section on the goldfinch × bullfinch, page 51).

This is probably the easiest hybrid to breed so is a very good pairing for first-time hybrid breeders.

Greenfinch × bullfinch

This cross has a grey back but is clear from any pencilling and when colour fed is richer and darker than the canary bullfinch cross. It is one of the most difficult hybrids to breed, even more so than the canary bullfinch cross (further details of this cross are contained in the section on bullfinches and their hybrids, page 53).

Of course, with this particular pairing the cock must be a greenfinch because no bullfinch cock has ever crossed with anything else. One major fault with this hybrid involves the head. Some examples tend to become very browy with age.

Northern greenfinch × bullfinch

As with all bullfinch hybrids, clear eggs are an issue, but the greenfinch bullfinch cross in particular seems to produce a high number of dead in shell young.

Greenfinch × redpoll

The greenfinch redpoll cross is again better bred using a redpoll cock and although it is quite easy to breed, this is not a popular hybrid because of its drab appearance. This hybrid looks prettier in its many colour variant forms, but it is still worth breeding to gain experience. A fuller description of this cross is given in the section on redpolls and their hybrids on page 63.

Greenfinch × crossbill

The greenfinch crossbill cross looks better when colour fed and has been bred in many different colours. It is a very nice, chunky bird that shows both parents well. Ron Phillips won Best Unflighted Hybrid at the 1999 National Exhibition at Telford with one of these hybrids. At the same event, Thundow and Lawson took the award for Best Hybrid with a lightly marked greenfinch mule. That was the year we moved the National to Telford, and I remember that,

Ron Phillips' greenfinch × crossbill

as Show Manager that year, I did not have the chance to see any of the birds. The change of venue was very stressful and thankfully, the following year we moved the event back to the National Exhibition Centre in Birmingham.

Greenfinch × chaffinch

The greenfinch chaffinch is a beautiful cross; another potential Best in Show winner, as long as it is large, steady and has a good depth of colour. It is well worth a try, even if few of this cross are achieved. This could be due to the greenfinch cock being less fertile than the hen. This cross, as with all chaffinch or bramblefinch crosses, requires large amounts of livefood, so transferring these birds to canaries for fostering can be a difficult decision as it is always difficult to get canaries to take livefood. You can mix some into the softfood, but unless the greenfinch chaffinch hybrids get enough their development will be retarded.

The best examples of this hybrid that I recall include a fine bird bred by Terry Roberts, which had great success on the show bench for many years. It never won the Supreme Award at the National although it took all other honours on more than one occasion. Another good example won G. Ridgway the award for Best Mule or Hybrid at the 1984 Scottish National. One outstanding bird belonged to a great bird keeper, the late John Broadbent. Every year he had a great team of mules and hybrids and he was a force to be reckoned with. His greenfinch chaffinch hybrid, which took the National Supreme Award in 1995, was the best I have seen.

The soft, velvet-like feather texture, depth of colour, broad yellow bars, size and confiding nature of this bird make it the perfect hybrid. John also won the Supreme Award in 1979 with a canary bullfinch cross. Both Terry and John won Best Hybrid at the National on numerous occasions.

Greenfinch × canary family

Redpoll × greenfinch

The greenfinch chaffinch hybrid can be bred in colour variant forms although to date I have only seen rather poor cinnamon varieties.

Greenfinch × linnet

Both the greenfinch and linnet are of a predominantly brown hue so there is little point in wasting valuable breeding stock on this pairing, other than for the achievement of breeding a hybrid. They are quite easy to breed and despite their normally muted colours, they can be enhanced in the many colour variant forms, possibly by using the greenfinch cock to produce colour variant hens. The cross is more easily achieved when using linnet cocks.

Greenfinch × siskin

A greenfinch siskin cross is a nice hybrid. I prefer these birds when they are not colour fed. As both birds are green, they have an excellent body colour. Their feather texture is also very good and they show both parents to the full. Using the smaller siskin cock and a greenfinch hen makes this cross easier to achieve.

Again, as with other crosses, colour variant forms can be produced. The green of both these birds is intensified in this hybrid whilst the markings of the siskin are subdued. The bird carries the cap of the siskin though it is not as black as in the parent. The breast and under belly are a rich, bold, bright green tinted with yellow running off at the vent to a buffish shade.

Very tame and accommodating, this hybrid takes after the greenfinch for the most part. Its song resembles that of the greenfinch but with a few of the siskin's lively notes. Compared to the colourful cock, hybrid hens are paler and duller in colour with a greyish tinge.

Greenfinch mule

Greenfinch × twite

As with the linnet, the twite's colouring is mainly brown so a greenfinch twite cross does not produce colourful hybrids. The main reason for attempting this cross is that they are quite easy to breed and so useful for gaining experience. The cross can be enhanced in its many colour variant forms, possibly by using the greenfinch cock to produce colour variant hens. However, this cross is easier to breed using the twite cock as the greenfinch cock is not so ready to interbreed.

Greenfinch × bramblefinch

Not often seen, the greenfinch bramblefinch hybrid is well worth producing although I prefer the greenfinch × chaffinch which is the prettier of the two as well as being slightly easier to breed.

Greenfinch cock

SISKINS AND THEIR HYBRIDS

Siskin (*Carduelis spinus*)

Status and distribution: Generally common but numbers are highly variable. Breeds in Ireland and Scotland, northern and western England, throughout Scandinavia except the extreme north and from the Massif Central and Vosges in France east across Europe to the Urals, reaching north to the White Sea in Russia. In the south, it breeds intermittently in the Pyrenees, Alps and Apennines, Sardinia, the Balkans, western Turkey and the Caucasus.

Northernmost birds are migratory, elsewhere a partial migrant or resident. Autumn migrations take place from September to early November, returning from late March to early May. Occasionally irruptive in winters of severe food shortage. Winter range extends south to the north Mediterranean coast and larger islands, north-west Africa, throughout Turkey and the Middle East, south to the Nile Valley in Egypt. Vagrants have been recorded in Iceland (where it has bred).

Habitat: Coniferous forest, especially in spruce, also larch and has adapted to living in commercial plantations in some areas. Also feeds in alder and birch, especially in winter. As well as forest, also found in more open woodland and heaths with scattered trees. In parts of western Europe has become a regular visitor to garden feeders.

The siskin cock is distinguished by its yellow and green plumage, black crown and bib. The hen is greyer with black pencilling on the flanks.

The clutch consists of four to six eggs, which hatch when they have been incubated for 12 days. The young

Siskin cock

leave the nest at approximately 13 to 17 days and are self supporting at about 24 days.

The siskin is a friendly and tame bird available in a few colour forms.

Siskin × greenfinch

These hybrids have an excellent body colour and feather texture showing their parentage to the full. They are very tame and accommodating and more easily bred with a siskin cock. Colour variant forms can be produced. For fuller information about this cross, see the greenfinch × siskin section on page 75.

Siskin × redpoll

There is little to recommend this cross other than the production of colour variant hens and to gain experience. However, if they are colour fed, yellow-feathered cocks can be worth showing as they have better colour and definition than buffs. As with all hybrids in the UK, the bird should be as large as possible and show both parents clearly. Colours should be well defined and rich.

The size of this hybrid depends on the redpoll variety used. Depth of colour also depends on the redpoll used. As the large redpoll species are normally not as dark as the smaller varieties, using large European redpolls will produce a larger hybrid but the colour will not be as good. It is a trade off, I'm afraid. The hybrid of this cross should be perfectly steady. Hens are of no use.

This hybrid is a cheerful little bird, full of life and activity. Cocks have a continuous chattering song. Hens' notes are very similar. In colour, hens are much paler and sober in appearance.

Siskin × goldfinch

This hybrid is not as colourful as one would expect but is very friendly and easy to breed.

A detailed description of this cross is included in the goldfinch × siskin section on page 40.

Siskin × linnet

The siskin linnet cross carries the distinct pencilling and markings of both parents but the green of the siskin is masked by the brown or ash – grey of the linnet, leading to an uninteresting hybrid.

Siskin × bullfinch

Victor Carr comments on the one and only siskin × bullfinch to be bred in his 1959 book *Mule and Hybrid Birds* (see page 59).

A reference to this particular bird being exhibited at Olympia in 1950 by A.B. Patterson of Kirkcaldy stated that the bird was 5th in its class and was accepted by some but not by all.

Siskin × twite

I have never seen an example of a siskin twite cross and doubt that it has ever been achieved. However, I assume that it would look just like the siskin linnet cross but darker and with a smaller beak. This should be an easy cross to produce, although whether it would be worth breeding is questionable.

Goldfinch × siskin

Siskin × canary

SISKIN × CROSSBILL

This cross has never been achieved, but it is well worth a try.

SISKIN × CHAFFINCH

In 1959, Victor Carr's notes in *Cage Birds* included a reference to the breeding of siskin chaffinch hybrids, which sadly did not survive. In this same report he mentioned his father, Percy Carr, had also bred a goldfinch chaffinch hybrid and sadly reported the death of the famous, light siskin mule belonging to J. E. Williams.

Siskin × goldfinch pairing

CROSSBILLS AND THEIR HYBRIDS

Common crossbill (*Loxia curvirostra*)

Status and distribution: The most widespread and numerous of the crossbills in the western Palearctic (Europe, Asia north of the Himalayas, and Africa north of the Sahara) but found intermittently over much of this area. Breeds in parts of Britain (especially southern Scotland and eastern and southern England), eastern France and the Alps, east across Europe to the Urals including much of non-Arctic Scandinavia. In the south, it breeds over much of Spain and the Pyrenees, Balearics, Corsica and Sardinia, Apennines and southern Italy, the Balkans south to northern Greece, parts of western, central and northern Turkey, Cyprus and the Caucasus. Also breeds in a limited area of north Africa from eastern Morocco to north-east Algeria and adjacent Tunisia and has bred in Israel. Many breeding populations are highly fluctuating and new areas are often colonised for a few years after an irruption but the main range has expanded slowly southwards in the 20th century.

Some birds are rather sedentary, others are partial migrants leaving breeding areas from June to August, but many are nomadic during the winter. Northern birds fairly regularly irrupt southwards, sometimes beyond range of southern breeders and remain to breed for a few years. Vagrants have been recorded in Iceland, the Faroes, Madeira, Canary Isles, Gibraltar, Libya, Lebanon and Syria.

Subspecies: Six races occur differing mainly in bill size and depth of colour of males. *Loxia curvirostra* occurs over

Scottish colour fed crossbill cock

much of Europe where the Scottish crossbill (*Loxia scotica*), which is very similar to the common crossbill, and parrot crossbill (*Loxia pytyopsittacus*) are also found. All three species are identical in plumage. The Scottish crossbill is larger than the common crossbill but smaller than the parrot crossbill. While further studies to clarify its taxonomic status are being carried out, the Scottish crossbill is treated by scientists as a distinct species. The paler *L. balearica* occurs on the Balearics, the duller and greyer *L. corsicana* on Corsica and *L. poliogyna* in north-west Africa with orange rather than red males and greyer females. All three of these races as well as *L. guillemardi* from Cyprus, are similar and have larger bills than *L. curvirostra.* The male of the Crimean subspecies *L. mariae* is brighter red and the female paler and greyer than *L. curvirostra.*

Other types of crossbill are the white-winged crossbill (*Loxia leucoptera*) and the red crossbill. The red crossbill is similar but lacks wing bars and has a larger bill.

Habitat: Coniferous forest, usually Scots pine, also larch and spruce and sometimes alder and birch. Mainly within forest but during irruptions often occurs in more open woodland and town parks. Frequently seen drinking from puddles and pools on the forest floor.

Description: Between 5¼ and 6½ inches in length (13-17 cm). Rusty red with white flecks, dark wings and tail. They have crossed mandibles as indicated by the name. Females are greyish with a dull yellow rump and underparts. Immature crossbills are duller and streaked.

A clutch is usually three to four eggs but sometimes five, incubated for about 12 to 14 days. Young leave the nest about 17 days after hatching and are self-supporting approximately two weeks later.

Although the crossbill is relatively new to hybridising, with just a few bred in the past, we have seen lots of crossbill mules and hybrids on the show bench in the last few years. It now seems to have been crossed with most of the common finches. However, it seems doubtful that we will ever see a cross with the siskin or lesser redpoll hen because of the size difference. But who knows?

Scottish crossbill hen

To the best of my knowledge, the first crossbill hybrid to be exhibited at a National Exhibition was in 1961 when it took the Supreme Award for best exhibit in the show. It was a crossbill greenfinch cross exhibited by W. McAllister of Scarborough.

In the section on the canary × crossbill (page 27), I described the bird that took the Supreme Award in 1964 and 1965 for J. Dalrymple. So within five years of the first crossbill hybrid being exhibited at the National, crossbill crosses had taken the top award in British aviculture three times.

More recently we have begun to see new crosses and colour variant crossbill hybrids. Several colour variant forms of crossbill hybrids, such as the satinette, cinnamon, silver and lutino, have been produced with canaries and greenfinches.

The size of crossbill hybrids is influenced by the type of crossbill used and when judging them this must be taken into account. The common crossbill is the smallest, followed by the Scottish and the largest is the parrot crossbill. Size is also influenced by the variety of finch with which the crossbill is paired. In my opinion, it will not be long before we see more being bred from the mealy redpoll, goldfinch and northern bullfinch but we have yet to see crossbill hybrids from the twite, siskin or hawfinch.

No species has ever hybridised with the hawfinch and I feel that the hawfinch cock will be like the bullfinch cock, in that it will never breed successfully with hens of other species. I think the best chance of producing hawfinch hybrids would be to cross a crossbill cock with a hawfinch hen.

Colour variant crossbills are being bred in Europe so it will not be long before we see these birds in the United

Redpoll × crossbill

Kingdom. This will give us an even larger range of colour variant hybrids. To date, I have only ever seen cinnamon. I believe that, like greenfinches and redpolls, the other colours will not be far behind as the crossbill gains popularity.

Crossbill × canary

This cross has been described in the section on the canary (see page 27). A bird not mentioned previously was exhibited by R. Partridge at the Scottish National of 1982 and won Best Mule or Hybrid.

Crossbill × greenfinch

This is relatively easy to breed and the youngsters tend to be nice and chunky, displaying the distinguishing features of both parents well. This is a hybrid that definitely benefits from being colour fed. An article in *Cage and Aviary Birds* by A. E. Cross in 1969 described his experience of breeding this cross. After four years of failure he won Best Unflighted Hybrid at the 1968 National.

Crossbill × goldfinch

This hybrid shows its parentage clearly. I assume this hybrid would be difficult to breed this way round, especially if the smaller English goldfinch is used with the larger parrot crossbill. So your best chance would be using a goldfinch cock to a crossbill hen.

Crossbill × linnet

This cross displays the chestnut back of the linnet and a red flush on the chest and head. The female hybrid shows no

Redpoll × crossbill at eight days old

red but is heavily pencilled on the breast, just like a linnet hen. It is also much larger than a linnet and has a slightly bulkier beak. Again, this cross is probably best achieved by using the smaller linnet cock to a crossbill hen.

Crossbill × redpoll

This cross has already been covered in the redpoll section and a fuller description is to be found on page 64. Normally it would be bred the other way round as the redpoll hen is so small, especially the lesser redpoll. I doubt whether a mating could be achieved from a crossbill cock with a redpoll hen, especially with the larger varieties of crossbill.

Crossbill × siskin

This cross has never successfully been done. The crossbill could be too big to achieve mating this way round, though it is worth trying using the siskin cock to crossbill hen. You may be the first to produce this hybrid although because the siskin cock has never bred with the bullfinch it may not breed with the crossbill either.

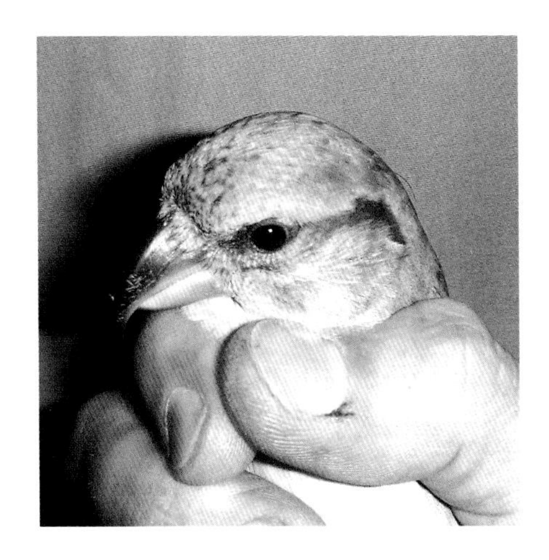

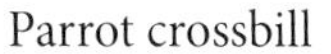
Parrot crossbill

Crossbill × bullfinch

This bird used to be very rare, but lots more crossbills are being kept and bred and are therefore now more often being used to produce hybrids. The crossbill bullfinch hybrids being bred at the moment all seem to be from northern bullfinch hens. For more information about this cross see the bullfinch hybrid section of this book (page 56).

Crossbill × bullfinch

LINNETS AND THEIR HYBRIDS

LINNET (*CARDUELIS CANNABINA*)

Status and distribution: Widespread and generally common. Breeds throughout the British Isles and from western France and Iberia east to the Urals reaching north to southern Norway, southern and eastern Sweden and central and southern Finland. In the south, occurs on Madeira and the Canary Islands, north-west Africa, most of the larger Mediterranean islands, Greece, Turkey and the Caucasus, and the Middle East.

Northern and eastern birds are migratory, leaving breeding areas in September to October to winter chiefly within range of southern breeders and along coast of north Africa, returning in late March to April. Elsewhere these birds are partial migrants or resident. Vagrants have been recorded north to Iceland and Lapland and south-east to Kuwait.

Subspecies: *Carduelis cannabina* occurs in Europe and north-west Africa with the Turkestan linnet, *C. bella*, occurring from central Turkey to the Caucasus and south to Israel. *C. bella* is paler above with very pale rump and pale grey crown and nape in the male. The Atlantic Isles have three races but they differ little from *C. cannabina*. Eastern Canarian *C. harterti* occurs in Lanzarote, Fuerteventura, Graciosa and Allegranza and is paler above and whiter on flanks. *C. meadewaldoi* from Palma, Hierro, Gomera, Tenerife and Gran Canaria and *C. nana* from Madeira are very similar.

Habitat: Open habitats with low shrubs and scattered trees, often found on moorland and heathland, along woodland edges, hedgerows and orchards, sometimes in large gardens.

Linnet cock

C. bella is found on rocky and scrub-covered mountain slopes. In winter, forms large flocks often with other finches and feeds on stubble fields and other cultivated areas, along shorelines and on waste ground.

This is a very popular finch to keep in a cage or aviary as it is sociable but not aggressive. Linnets hybridise readily but never seems to tame easily, being always flighty. The cock has a red

Sexing linnets
Males have a larger white area on their flights than females.

chest while the hen shows no red at all.

Eggs hatch 12 days after incubation begins, young leave the nest at approximately 11 days and are self supporting at about 21 days old.

Linnet × crossbill

This hybrid displays the chestnut back of the linnet and a red flush on the chest and head. The female hybrid shows no red but is heavily pencilled on the breast, just like a linnet hen. It is also much larger than a linnet and has a slightly bulkier beak. Further details are included in the crossbill hybrid section (page 88).

Linnet × siskin

This bird carries the distinct pencilling and markings of both parents but the green of the siskin is masked by the brown or ash-grey of the linnet which makes this cross rather uninteresting. As this hybrid is generally difficult to breed concentrating on a different, easier to achieve and more colourful cross would be more worthwhile.

Linnet × greenfinch

This cross is quite easy to breed and more useful for gaining breeding experience than producing colourful hybrids. However, it can be enhanced in the many colour variant forms, possibly by using the greenfinch cock to produce colour variant hens. It is easier to breed this way round.

Linnet × redpoll

This cross is quite easy to breed either way round and again is mainly useful for breeding experience. The most attractive part of this hybrid is the breast colour when properly colour fed. This bird is enhanced in its many colour variant forms, possibly by using the redpoll cock to produce colour variant hens.

Linnet × twite

This hybrid has no real purpose. The twite resembles the linnet in many ways so the bird looks like a linnet with a twite's beak.

Linnet × bramblefinch

According to Victor Carr, in his book *Mule and Hybrid Birds*, this hybrid has been hatched but never reared.

Linnet × chaffinch

This hybrid has never been produced as far as I am aware, although it could be possible, especially if the linnet × bramblefinch has been hatched.

Linnet × bullfinch

Along with the goldfinch bullfinch hybrid, this is probably the easiest bullfinch hybrid to produce. This bird does not steady down easily and some lack the red or orange tint associated with the cross. Some are also too dark. To be successful on the show bench it is not just a matter of producing a hybrid, it must be a yellow cock. Unfortunately, nothing else will do.

Linnet × goldfinch

The linnet goldfinch cross is another hybrid that is as easy to breed as any hybrid ever is. Its colour is that of a good-coloured linnet with a red blaze and yellow wing bars. A full blaze on this cross is rare and it is normally full on the forehead only. This hybrid shows both parents well and has an excellent song.

Linnet × crossbill cock

Linnet × canary family

TWITES AND THEIR HYBRIDS

TWITE (*CARDUELIS FLAVIROSTRIS*)

Status and distribution: In the Western Palearctic it occurs in two widely separated areas: in coastal areas of the north-west and in the region of the Caucasus. In north-western Europe it breeds in the Faroes, the north and west of the British Isles and from southern Norway north in coastal areas to Varangerfjord and the Kola Peninsula. This population is resident or partially migratory in the south and fully migratory north of the Arctic Circle. Migrants leave breeding areas in late September to October to winter from southern England to Denmark, southern Sweden and the Baltic coasts to southern Finland, returning in March and April. Also recorded further south in Spain, southern France, Hungary and Romania. The eastern population breeds in east and south-east Turkey and throughout the Caucasus, mainly an altitudinal migrant extending its range in winter to Central Turkey. Recorded as a vagrant on Sicily.

Subspecies: Nominate race (*C. flavirostris*) occurs in Fenno-Scandia replaced by warmer brown *C. pipilans* in British Isles, but the two are very similar in worn plumage. Caucasian race *C. brevirostris* is more distinct, paler above and on face with pale pink rump and broad dark streaks on sides of an otherwise whitish breast.

Habitat: In north-western Europe breeds on open moorland, usually coastal, sometimes in mountains, in areas of rocky grassland and dwarf birch. Winters in lower, often coastal areas of open land with weeds and scattered rocks and bushes, sometimes on pastures and in reed beds. Caucasian birds breed on high plateaux, on scree slopes and cliffs, in alpine meadows and sparsely vegetated hillsides. In winter generally in lower areas of plains and valleys.

The twite is very closely related to the linnet and is also called the mountain linnet. The main difference between the twite and the linnet is the beak. Twites have very short beaks and no pink chest. Cock twites have a red rump but the twite hen does not. Other than that the sexes are simi-

Twite

lar. The twite may also be a close relative of the redpoll.

Twites are ready nesters in confinement, so it seems strange that very few twite hybrids have ever been produced. I have only found reference to the twite having hybridised with the redpoll, linnet and greenfinch, crosses which have only been achieved once to my knowledge.

The linnet has crossed with most species and so has the redpoll, so perhaps the twite is not as closely related at it seems or perhaps we have just neglected the twite in our hybridising attempts. There certainly seems no reason why the twite could not be crossed with the bullfinch, goldfinch, crossbill and siskin.

Twite × linnet

The twite resembles the linnet in many ways so this cross would look like a linnet with a twite's beak. The only cross that I know of was exhibited at Olympia in 1959.

Twite × siskin

I have never seen this cross and doubt it has ever been done. However, I assume that it would look just like the siskin × linnet but darker and with a smaller beak.

Twite × greenfinch

Again, both being similar, brown-based birds, there is little point in wasting valuable breeding stock on this pairing, other than for the achievement of breeding a hybrid. They are quite easy to breed and may be enhanced in the many colour variant forms, possibly by using the greenfinch cock to produce colour variant hens. However, it would be easier to breed using the twite cock because the greenfinch cock is not so ready to interbreed.

Twite × bullfinch

To date, this hybrid has never been bred but I can see no reason why not. So it is well worth a try.

Twite × goldfinch

This cross has been produced on at least two occasions although I am not sure which way round (see the goldfinch × twite section on page 42). Why so few have been bred is a mystery. The twite is called the mountain linnet and is closely related to the linnet and to the redpoll. As both of these species cross well, this hybrid is very much worth a try.

Twite × redpoll

The twite × redpoll looks like the redpoll × linnet, but with a smaller beak. Its main use is for the production of colour variant hens. This cross is not often bred so it could be difficult to achieve, though I doubt it. I have seen this cross only once and that was in Europe.

CHAFFINCHES AND THEIR HYBRIDS

CHAFFINCH (*FRINGILLA COELEBS*)

Status and distribution: Widespread and generally abundant in the British Isles, and from western France and Iberia east to the Urals and north to beyond the Arctic Circle in Scandinavia and south to the Canary Isles, north-west Africa and north Libya, the Mediterranean islands, Turkey and the Caucasus and the Middle East. Most Swedish and Finnish birds are migratory as are those occurring from eastern Poland eastwards. In winter, becomes more widespread around the Mediterranean and in the Middle East.

Vagrants have been recorded in Iceland.

Subspecies: Many subspecies have been recognised, differing mainly in the plumage of the male. Most European birds are very similar with *F. coelebs* occurring over much of Europe, *F. gengleri* in the British Isles with more brick-red underparts and *F. schiebeli* from Crete, paler below with a pale pink throat.

North African and Atlantic Isle birds are more distinct. *F. africana* from Morocco to western Tunisia and *F. cyrenaica* are blue-grey on the head and nape, olive-green on the back and rump and pale pink below. *F. spodiogenys* from eastern Tunisia and north-west Libya is similar but has a blue rump and more white in the wings. *F. tintillon* from Gran Canaria, Tenerife and Gomera has very dark blue upperparts, a green rump and pale orange underparts. *F. ombriosa* from Hierro is similar but greener on the back and paler below and *F. palmae* from La Palma is all blue above and whitish below. The Madeiran subspecies *F. maderensis* is blue on the head, nape and lower

Chaffinch cock

back, greenish on the mantle and rump with a pale orange throat and breast and whitish belly and flanks. The Azorean *F. moreletti* is similar but paler blue above with a blue rump and more extensive orange below.

Habitat: Coniferous, mixed and deciduous woodland, farmland with hedgerows and copses, parks and large gardens. Atlantic Isle birds live mainly in laurel and pine forests.

Chaffinches should be treated as softbills during the breeding season. The eggs hatch approximately 13 days after incubation begins. Young leave the nest at 14 days old and are self supporting at 28 days. The chaffinch cock has only ever crossed with the bramblefinch.

Chaffinch × bramblefinch

Whether bred using the bramblefinch cock or the chaffinch cock, the cross is almost identical and it is only the smaller amounts of white on the wing bars and the slightly smaller head of the bramblefinch that give some clue to the male parentage. But even these distinctions are not infallible and one needs great experience to even hazard a guess as to which way round this cross was produced.

CHAFFINCH × GREENFINCH

Cage and Aviary Birds reported in 1956 that B. Minshall of Shropshire had bred a chaffinch greenfinch hybrid and that this had already been recorded in 1912 (Ron Phillips, *History of the Scottish British Bird and Mule Club*). It is still worthy of note and a credit to the breeder but I wonder if the report had the birds written the wrong way round?

Greenfinch × chaffinch

Greenfinch × chaffinch family

BRAMBLINGS AND THEIR HYBRIDS

Brambling (*Fringilla montifringilla*)

Status and distribution: Breeds throughout Norway and in all but the southernmost parts of Sweden and Finland, in Estonia and across northern Russia east to the Urals. An isolated population breeds in the Alps in Switzerland and northern Italy and the brambling has bred in Iceland, north-central Scotland, the Netherlands, Germany and Denmark. A migratory species with autumn passage mainly in mid-September to October, sometimes November, with most birds moving south or south-west through Europe. Widespread in winter throughout Europe south of the breeding range occurring west to Iberia and south to the Mediterranean, Turkey and the Middle East. Return passage takes place from March to mid-May. Vagrants have been recorded in Iceland and the Faroes and have bred in both. Also recorded in the Canaries, Madeira, Cyprus and north Africa, Jordan and Iraq.

Habitat: Breeds in open coniferous forest, birch woodland and riverine willows and winters along woodland edges close to open farmland and especially stubble fields. In some areas large numbers gather in autumn and winter in beechwoods to feed on beechmast. Also fond of hornbeam seeds.

Bramlings or bramblefinches become very territorial in the breeding season. The only cross produced so far using the bramblefinch cock is the bramblefinch ×

chaffinch. The eggs hatch approximately 14 days after incubation begins. Young leave the nest at 14 days old and are self supporting at 28 days.

The cock is much brighter than the hen, having a head mottled with brown on black. In the breeding season the cock assumes a completely black head, mantle, wings and tail. The hen has duller brown upperparts with a buff-grey head and is generally paler in colour.

Bramblefinch × chaffinch

For details of this cross, the only one to have been achieved to date with the bramblefinch, see the section on the chaffinch × bramblefinch on page 102.

Bramblefinch cock

OTHER HYBRIDS

Other possibilities

There are many hybrids yet to be achieved. The following are just a few that have not yet been produced to my knowledge: siskin × bullfinch; twite × bullfinch; twite × crossbill; siskin × crossbill; crossbill × chaffinch; crossbill × bramblefinch; bullfinch cock × any finch; siskin × chaffinch; siskin × twite; bramblefinch × greenfinch; chaffinch cock × any finch other than bramblefinch; any hawfinch cross.

Many have been claimed and each year one hears of something new. If you know that one of those on the list has already been bred, please let me have the details.

Only a few varieties of softbill have ever been crossed, so there is tremendous scope here. Breeding any of the hybrids listed would cause quite a lot of interest in the fancy. Perhaps you could be the first!

Softbill hybrids

Hybrids produced from softbills are rarely seen on the show bench, but a few have been bred over the years either on purpose or by chance. That means there is plenty of scope to be first to produce a new cross. One of the main reasons why so few softbill hybrids have been produced could be that there are currently few softbill breeders in Britain. However, softbills are becoming more popular again so we may see a few more hybrids. I hope so.

Below are described the only softbill hybrids that I know for certain have been produced.

Fieldfare × blackbird

This cross was produced for the first time in 1978. Both parents can be seen in this cross.

Blackbird × songthrush

This hybrid has been bred only a few times. I believe the first one appeared in the 1930s and, by all accounts, it resembled a melanistic thrush, but on closer examination the male blackbird could be seen. This hybrid has also been bred by Bernard Howlett. I saw his bird at the London and Home Counties Show in 2003.

Yellow × pied wagtail

The first time this cross was achieved was in 1958, bred by J. Spinks of Colchester. Several young were bred from the same pair. The parentage was far from obvious as the beautiful colours of the yellow were superseded by those of the pied. These birds were exhibited at the National

Song thrush × blackbird

Bred by Bernard Howlett.

Exhibition, Olympia in 1958. The breeder had plenty of witnesses to prove that they were genuine hybrids and not just mis-coloured pied wagtails, and the birds were accepted without any doubt.

Grey × pied wagtail

In 1964 J. Craig showed one of these at the Scottish National.

Whinchat × stonechat

This hybrid clearly shows its parentage.

Ring ouzel × mistlethrush

This hybrid too shows its parentage clearly.

Ring ouzel

SHOW STANDARDS
(Points awarded for excellence of show qualities)

Light mules		
Size	To be of good size, compatible with parents' size.	15
Shape	To be of stout, cone shape, with broad, bold head, and close-fitting wings and tail.	15
Colour	To be naturally deep and rich in colour, and when colour fed to be considerably intensified.	10
Markings	To be distinctly characteristic of both parents; the clearer the plumage the better.	20
Quality	Plumage to exhibit the smoothest and glossiest surface possible throughout.	15
Condition	To be sound in condition in every part.	10
Steadiness	The bolder and firmer the stand on the perch the better.	10
Staging	To be shown in clean condition and in a clean cage.	5
	Total points	100
Dark mules and British hybrids		
Size	The larger the better; compatible with the size of the parents.	15
Shape	To be of stout, cone shape, with broad, bold head.	10
Colour	To be rich, deep and distinct.	20
Markings	To show the chief characteristics, markings and colour of both parents distinctly and well blended.	15
Quality	The plumage to possess the smoothest and glossiest surface possible.	15
Condition	To be sound in condition in every part.	10
Steadiness	To be bold, firm, steady and fearless on the perch.	10
Staging	To be shown in clean condition and in a clean cage.	5
	Total points	100

SHOW CAGES FOR MULES AND HYBRIDS
(For the guidance of cage manufacturers)

Size No. 2	
For lesser redpoll, mealy redpoll, siskin, goldfinch, linnet, twite and all mules and British hybrids which do not exceed the size of these finches and the redpoll × bullfinch.	
English pattern	Length 11″ × height 9½″ × depth 4½″
Scottish pattern	Length 10″ × height 9½″ × depth 4½″
Both patterns	No. 14 gauge wires set at ⅝″ between centres. The drinking hole should be ¾″ in diameter for redpolls and siskins and ⅞″ in diameter for other birds.
Bottom rail	1½″ high.
Top Rail (shaped)	1″ at the outside, sloping to ½″ at the centre.
Perches	¼″ diameter for redpolls and siskins, and ⅜″ diameter for others. Perch centres, measured outside on the back of the cage, 2½″ high from the base, with 3½″ space between them and set equidistant from either end.
Colour	Front wires, top and bottom rails and inside cage is Brolac Georgian Green. Drinker is green to match. Outside is black.

Size No. 3	
For bullfinch, chaffinch, bramblefinch, greenfinch, reed bunting, yellowhammer, goldfinch, greenfinch, linnet and twite mules and British hybrids not exceeding the size of the buntings.	
English pattern	Length 12″ × height 10″ × depth 4½″
Scottish pattern	Length 11″ × height 10″ × depth 5″

Both patterns	No. 14 gauge wires set at ¾″ between centres. Drinking hole should be 1⅛″ diameter.
Bottom rail	1½″ high.
Top Rail (shaped)	1″ at the outside, sloping to ½″ at the centre.
Perches	½″ diameter, perch centres measured outside on the back of the cage 2¾″ high from the base with 4″ space between them and set equidistant from either end.
Colour	Front wires, top and bottom rails and inside cage, Brolac Georgian Green. Drinker is green to match. Outside is black.

Size No. 4	
For hawfinch, crossbill, corn bunting, snow bunting, and lapland bunting and all mules and other British hybrids similar in size to the hardbills in this category.	
	Length 14″ × height 12″ × depth 6½″
	No. 14 gauge wires set at 1″ between centres. Drinking hole should be 1¼″ diameter.
Bottom rail	2″ high.
Top Rail (shaped)	1½″ at the outside, sloping to ¾″ at the centre.
Colour	Front wires, top and bottom rails and inside cage is Brolac Georgian Green. Drinker is green to match. Outside is black.

Show cage

Size No. 5	
For dunnock.	
	Length 16″ × height 13″ × depth 8″†
Colour	Black outside including wire fronts with white interior. Food and water vessels inside the cage.

Size No. 6	
For blackbird, song thrush, starling.	
	Length 18″ × height 15″ × depth 12″†
Colour	Black outside including wire fronts with white interior. Food and water vessels inside the cage.

Size No. 8	
For jackdaw, jay, magpie.	
	Length 30″ × height 20″ × depth 14″†
Colour	Black outside including wire fronts with white interior. Food and water vessels inside the cage.

† These are minimum sizes.

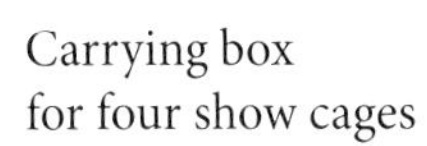

Carrying box
for four show cages

MY WAY

There is no single, 'correct' way to keep birds because every breeder uses slightly different techniques.

The following chapters are intended to show how I keep birds in the hope that it will help others who share my interest. I have kept birds all my life and birds will always play an important part in my life.

If you wish to keep or breed birds, the thing to do is to listen and watch how other fanciers do it, pick out what suits you, and then develop your own way. Do not keep swapping and changing. Find a method that suits you and stick to it.

My shed is quite large, but just remember many a fine hybrid has been bred in a double breeding cage or in an outhouse where no other birds are kept. Keep only the number of birds that you can cope with and start off with just a few. Walk before you run. It is a hobby, after all, not a chore. Do not be put off by seeing large setups in bird magazines and books. Lots of bird keepers only have 8ft × 6ft sheds. There are times when I wish I still did.

Remember that keeping livestock is a 365 days-a-year task. You can never miss a single day. Even on Christmas Day, your birds need to eat and drink. Consider who will look after them if you are away on holiday or ill? Having friends in the hobby helps because you can look after each others' birds to allow for holidays.

It is tempting to keep buying stock but, before you do, think of the extra work – don't be tempted to overstretch yourself to the point where you no longer enjoy your hobby.

MY BIRD ROOM

I decided to double the size of my bird room in January 2003. The principles I used to create this extension can also be used if you are building a new shed from scratch. The pictures below show the stages and progress of the project. This was the 5th bird room that I have built, so I wanted to make sure I got it right this time.

The first job is to decide on what size of shed is adequate for the number of birds you require. Build it as large as possible at the start or allow room for expansion at a later date when you need more space and funds allow.

Before the extension was built my shed measured 12 feet by eight feet. At its lowest point it was 7ft 6in high and in the middle it measured 9ft 6in high. The reason for the extra height was so that I could add a window in the back panel above the cages for extra natural light. Also, having a lowest height of 7ft 6in gave me room for an extra row of cages. I need a small step to reach the highest cages, but I only use them during the breeding season when I need the extra space. This may be too high for some but another advantage of the extra height is to help to disperse the heat in summer so that the shed stays much cooler.

Base ready for shed extension

The new part of the shed has 74 cages spread over three sides. The cages in the bottom row are two feet in height, 16 inches deep and two feet

New extension being fitted

and six inches wide. There are three on each side and four across the back, with sides that can be removed to create longer cages. The side cages can be opened up to approximately 6ft 6in and the back cage can be opened up to approximately 7ft 6in.

On top of these cages are 65 canary-type cages, each 13 inches deep with 15″ x 12″ cage fronts that can be opened up to create double, treble and quadruple cages. Having different sized cages helps me to provide accommodation suitable for different species. Crossbills, for example, need more room than canaries or siskins.

Building the extension

The first job in creating the extension was to pave the area with concrete slabs. To create a floor raised above ground level, 12 pillars of house bricks were then built to a height of four courses, and a frame made from 3″ × 2″ section timber was constructed to carry and strengthen the floor. Damp proof membrane was attached to the top surface of every pillar where the timber touched the brickwork. This

Shed built off the ground

is to stop rising damp from rotting the wood. The timber used was tanalised-treated to protect it from rotting.

The wooden frame was then attached to the pillars using galvanised joist hangers. These were bent and dropped into the centre of the pillars which were then filled with concrete. The final job at this stage was to construct the steps to allow easy access to the shed. It is not essential to raise your shed above ground level, but I feel that it stops vermin, such as mice, rats and stoats, from gaining access. Also the airflow underneath it prevents the floor from rotting.

Movement of fresh air around the entire shed is created by having louvered windows in the back wall and a mesh door in the front wall. This is complemented by having air vents, nine inches by four inches, fixed to the back wall; two low and two high. This arrangement ensures that fresh air is kept moving through the shed.

The next stage was the erection of the shed. My shed is built with tongue and groove log lap, with 3″ × 2″ framing for extra strength. The log lap is 3/4″ thick so no insulation is necessary.

Louver windows and air vents

The original shed was six years old and not one joint has opened up in that time, but the roof needed to be re-felted. This was done when the extension was added. The next job was to remove the front of the shed, add the floor and screw it to the timber frame. Then the new sides, which were fitted with windows to bring even more light into the interior, were added. The shed front was then replaced but set eight feet further forward than previously.

The next stage was to fix the two new roof panels. Inside the roof there are three beams to carry the weight, especially important when there is six inches of snow on the roof, as there was when the room was being constructed. The next job was the guttering and repainting of the shed so that it all looked like a single construction. The outside was now complete.

Most shed-making companies will erect the shed at no extra cost. It is worth ordering your shed in the winter when the shed companies are quiet; you will get a better deal. Also it can be completed in time for the coming breeding season. My shed now measures 16ft × 12ft inside.

Remember to plan the inside before you order your shed, so your cages will fit exactly from edge to edge. It will make the overall internal appearance much more pleasing. Your shed will cost you no more if it is built a few inches longer or shorter to fit your cages exactly.

The new extension was now sealed. The next job was

Just the roof to fit

Marley tiled floor

the electrics. The shed required three six feet fluorescent tubes, two dimmable bulbs to act as night lights, or just to provide dimmer lights. This gives the facility to turn off the fluorescent lights and dim the shed, to allow the birds to roost before putting them in total darkness. There is also a timer to allow the lights to switch on in the morning and off at night. Three double sockets were installed at convenient points.

The next job was the floor covering. I used marley tiles because these are easy to clean. Before installing the tiles the tongue and groove boards of the floor were covered with thin plywood sheet, to stop the tiles from cracking where the floorboards meet. The tiles were glued in position.

Because I had birds in the shed already, I was careful to use an adhesive that that did not give off a heavy vapour.

The guttering needed to be extended and the outside of the shed needed to be coated with a quality shed treatment. The product I used was Ronseal shed and fence guard. A most useful addition to any shed is a sink. Cleaning is a chore that has to be undertaken daily. The

The finished product

addition of a sink makes this job much easier and less time consuming.

After two years the shed's standard roofing felt had started to leak around the clout nails. So I decided to change the roofing material. After months of investigation, I eventually chose felt tiles. These are better than standard roofing felt because they allow movement. Roofing felt is applied and nailed with clout nails but the shed roof expands in the warmer weather in the summer and contracts in the colder months. This means that the area of felt around each clout nail stretches and loosens. Water soon begins to seep into the room around these nail holes. The felt tiles come in one metre sections and measure 300mm (12in) deep. The first row is applied with mastic using a standard mastic gun. The mastic is applied to the top and bottom edges, approximately 1in from the edge. The tile is then put in place and clout nails applied at the top edge, again approximately 1in from the top. When the first row is completed the next

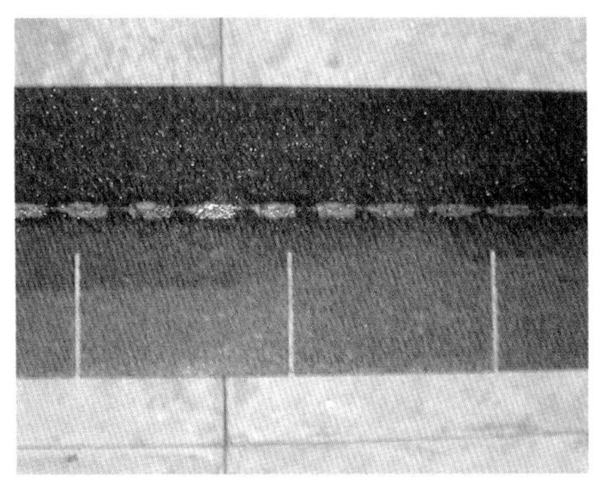

Felt roofing shingle

row is started by overlapping the first row by 50 per cent and applying the mastic in the same way.

This procedure is repeated until the roof is completely covered. No clout nails will be visible and even when the shed expands and contracts the tiles will move with the roof. Covering a roof with these tiles works out more expensive than roofing felt, but if you consider the 10 year, guaranteed, leak-free period, it is well worth the extra investment. Because each row of tiles overlaps the next row by 50 per cent, the roof is doubly protected and also looks better. Tiles are more attractive than felt and add a feature to your garden. Each pack of 17 tiles covers approximately 2.77 square metres (approx. 9ft square), depending on the brand used.

Roof completed

New breeding cages awaiting cage fronts

Left-hand side with sink area and varied cage sizes

HOUSING

Hybrids have been bred in all sorts of conditions even in pet budgie cages, either by chance or design. However, in my experience using standard cages gives the best chance of producing canary hybrids with finch cocks.

I have large breeding cages that are six feet long, 18 inches deep and 18 inches high. These can be divided if necessary to produce four, 18 inch cages. Using this method, I can always insert wire mesh dividers to stop aggressive cocks from upsetting their hens and damaging eggs or nests.

This method of dividing cages also allows me to separate the young mules when they are weaned and still leave plenty of room for the adult pair without too much interference. It also means you do not have to handle young birds too soon, which avoids stress. This size of cage suits most common hybrid pairings, such as goldfinch, greenfinch, linnet, siskin and also bullfinch hens. Crossbills will also accept this size cage, but care is needed otherwise they will strip the wood in the cages in no time at all. Always give crossbills a good supply of fruit tree or willow branches and pine cones. These help to keep them occupied and so cages will last longer.

I find these cages give me more control over the birds and allow less outside interference than aviaries. Aviaries do have their uses for birds like crossbills, chaffinches and bramblefinches and are required for insectivorous species.

Generally, unless your breeding birds were bred in cages as mine were, you will probably find it possible to breed more hybrids of any type in aviaries.

Right hand side of shed

AVIARIES

The most useful aviaries for breeding hardbills or hybrids measure two metres deep by one metre wide by two metres high. Obviously the exact dimensions depend on the size of the birds you decide to keep, but aviaries of this size are adequate for all finches.

The back wall of the aviary should be solid. The sides can be solid or double wired with a gap of at least 50mm between the mesh panels. The roof should be at least half solid starting from the back. The front half of the roof can be covered with wire mesh or plastic to allow plenty of light. Aviaries, like cages, should be light not dark because plenty of natural daylight is important when young are being reared.

Young birds need to be fed often and this can only happen when there is sufficient daylight. Chicks starved of light in the early stages of their development never make good, strong, healthy birds. If necessary, use artificial light but never allow the lights to switch off instantly. If the hen happens to be off the nest, the young will chill overnight and die. It is worth buying a timed dimmer

that has a 30 minute slow switch off. As the light gradually dims, the female will get back on the eggs or young naturally, just as she would in the wild when night falls.

Safety porch

All aviaries should have a safety porch to prevent birds from escaping. Birds do get out from time to time. Choosing not to have a safety porch is a false economy as the value of even one pair of birds lost from the aviary is probably greater than the cost of installing the porch. The height of the door into an aviary should always be less than the full height of the aviary. This is because birds often fly overhead as someone enters. If there are a few feet of mesh above the door, this will stop escapees. As you will not be going into your aviary on a daily basis, bending to enter should not be a problem.

Duplex plastic sheeting is very strong and allows plenty of light.

The aviary should be built on a solid foundation, preferably raised to help stop the wood from rotting by keeping it above the soil. Raising the aviary also helps prevent predators from tunnelling underneath. The base of the aviary should therefore rest on brick walls built to a height of not less than 12in and extending at least another 12in beneath the soil.

Duplex sheeting

All nest sites should be posi-

Feeding stations

tioned at the same height and under the covered area. Provide plenty of nest sites so that pairs have a choice. Only the under cover area should have any provision for nest sites to prevent birds trying to build their nest in the open where it will be subject to wind, rain and predators.

Feeding stations should be built so that you have easy access to them from the safety porch area and they have sufficient cover to protect them from the rain and avoid outside contamination.

Aviaries built in one metre sections can be extended as time and money allow, depending on the space you have available. In suburban areas it is wise to build the roof with trip wires to stop cats from climbing onto the roof of the aviary. This is always a problem because cats are attracted to the birds and are very difficult to stop. Fixing a net 200mm above the roof might help as cats will usually only stand on solid surfaces.

Aviary built from concrete fence posts

The floor of the aviary can be of solid concrete, gravel or

soil. All do the job well but, personally, I prefer concrete or slabs. These floors are easy to clean and hose down with disinfectant or Jeyes fluid. Birds will pick over soil floors and although they at first gain useful nutrients, over the years the soil becomes contaminated. Seed dropped by the birds or falling from feeding stations will germinate and the build up of bacteria will eventually become lethal. I know of keepers who have had to dig out two feet of soil to try to eradicate the problem of contaminated aviaries.

The same applies to gravel. Gravel can be hosed off and treated with Jeyes fluid but eventually germinated seed will cover the floor. Then it will become difficult to clean although it can be raked over, replenished or replaced. The damp and humid conditions under the gravel are a perfect breeding ground for bacteria.

Gravel floors help avoid contamination

NESTING, RINGING, BREEDING

Nesting sites

I use three types of nest sites for breeding in my shed; the first is for British bird pairs and the second and third are for mule and hybrid pairs where the female is a finch.

The standard bowl is for my canaries and mule pairs where the female is a canary.

Canary nest pans

Finches require a more natural nest bowl but canaries are less fussy and a standard bowl is adequate.

For canaries, I use plastic bowls with holes in the bottom for ventilation and a felt liner. I glue in the liner with four dots of silicone sealer and leave overnight to dry. Fixed like this, the liner pulls out easily after the breeding cycle. It pays to spray the liner with a good anti-mite spray.

Behind the nest bowl I fit a six inch square of plastic tile between the bowl and the cage. This helps to keep the cage side clean from the faeces that the young deposit.

Nest sites fixed under roof cover

One type of finch

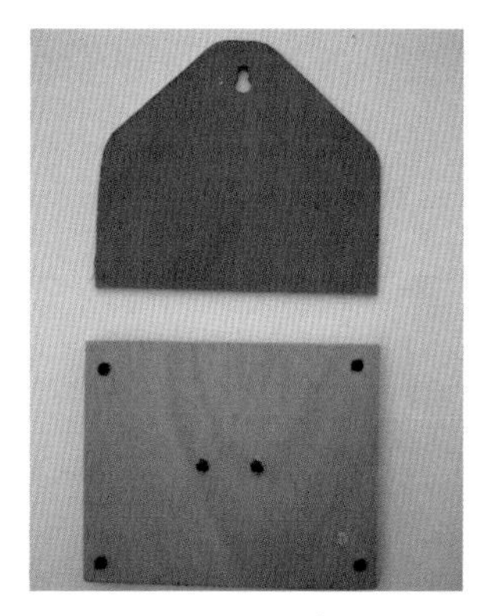

Nest support frame

nest site that I use requires a piece of 4mm thick plywood, 130mm wide by 115mm high, sloped on both sides with a screw slot in the centre top, and a piece of 10mm thick ply, 130mm wide by 100mm deep, drilled with holes in each corner and two holes in the centre 30mm apart. These are glued and panel pinned together.

Then, using a standard wicker basket, fix the basket by bending the piece of wire that comes with the basket into a 'U' shape. Push it through the nest basket and through the two centre holes in the base of the wooden frame and twist them tightly from underneath using pliers. Then push a small branch of ever-green shrub into each of the four corner holes. In the picture shown, I have used fragments of artificial Christmas tree. These can be washed and reused year after year.

The second finch nest site consists of a half open wire box with hooks at the top to fix it to the cage front. The hooks make it easy for me to lift the nest site down to check eggs and ring young finches. At the front, inside the box, I fix a wicker basket. Each wicker basket comes complete with a wire hook which is threaded through the bottom of the wire box and twisted. Any excess wire is cut off so that the birds do not get caught up on it. This type of nest site helps the female ward off any unwanted advances from the male whilst she is sitting on eggs as the nest is protected from the cock on all sides and from above. This means the female only has the front opening to protect. Over-fit cocks will disturb females whilst they are broody and this type of nest site gives the hen more security. Always give finch hens a choice of nest site and type of nest. I always offer each pair at least two sites. Canary hens are not so fussy, but I still offer two sites even though I only ever use the standard nest pans.

Wire nest cage

Nesting material

To line nests, I use moss from the lawn, washed and treated with Duramitex (an anti-mite spray) and dried. I also use proprietary pet nest material and fine grasses.

Ringing

In England, it is not necessary to ring young mules or hybrids from parents on Schedule 3. However, if either parent is listed on Schedule 4, they must be closed ringed and registered with DEFRA. For exact details see the table on the DEFRA website (www.defra.gov.uk) or ask for the current documents for schedules of ringing requirements,

Young British birds for sale must be ringed

from the British Bird Council. I have not listed which species are on which schedule as species may be moved from time to time from one schedule to the other. So please keep up to date with the current legislation.

British finches must be ringed with official, closed rings before they can be sold or exhibited. Official rings carry a unique number to identify each bird. Ring sizes carry an identifying letter and particular sizes are legally required depending on the species. The ring size requirement can change at any time, so always check that you are using the correct size.

Rings also show the year a bird was ringed which is useful information when purchasing stock. Never buy birds that are not ringed. This is illegal. Even when a bird is ringed, check the ring closely when purchasing a bird. Make sure the ring is marked with the right letter of the alphabet for the species. If a ring shows any damage, is misshapen or looks as if it is very thin on the inside, refuse the bird. If the seller is not prepared to let you check the ring before purchase, then refuse to buy it. Birds that are unringed can be given as a gift provided no money changes hands.

If the bird is on

Schedule 4, make sure that the registration document is given to you with the bird, just as you would demand a car registration document when buying a vehicle. These birds are registered with the owner and DEFRA must be sent details of the new owner. Both seller and buyer are required to send the relevant forms to DEFRA to register the change of ownership. There is a small charge for this.

Lutino greenfinch (red eyes)

Always keep a record of all ring numbers and where all your birds have come from and the date of purchase. Ring numbers and date of breeding should also be kept for birds you breed yourself. Never buy birds from car boot sales or stalls unless you can be sure that you know the person is honest and trustworthy. Make sure you have a full and accurate address for the seller.

It is advisable to join the British Bird Council as soon as you decide to keep British or European species and read up on the legislation that applies to keeping birds. Further information about buying birds is also available.

Most bird breeders are honest but, as in any other walk of life there is always the occasional exception. If you stay within the law you will have a great hobby and no worries.

Wild birds are exactly that, wild! They do not breed well in captivity, they never tame very well and some die through stress. As a result they are definitely not as good as aviary-bred specimens. Aviary-bred greenfinches and redpolls are excellent examples. They have been line bred to such an extent that they are much larger than their wild counterparts and only these bigger, tamer birds will do well on the show bench. Such birds are now bred in large quantities and in many colour variant forms so the supply outweighs the demand. Greenfinches and redpolls are the best species for a beginner to breed in order to gain experience.

Breeding

There are no hard and fast rules about breeding hybrids and the absolute novice stands just as much chance as any champion.

The pair must, of course, be compatible. Birds should be put together before becoming too fit. I always put my birds together in late December and they are left together until mid-April when they are split for two weeks. At this time, I add the nest sites and then reintroduce the pairs.

Birds like greenfinches, linnets and redpolls come into condition early. Birds like crossbills need to be held back as they are ready to breed in February. Siskins and goldfinches are ready about one month later.

I start to increase the light in the shed gradually from February until the lights are on for a full 16 hours a day. Most bird rooms with a solid roof are always in semi-darkness, so using fluorescent lighting will help birds come into condition earlier. If birds are fit they will breed, so food should be increased, not only in quantity but also in quality. I feed multi-vitamins at this time as well as condition seeds, wild seeds, greenfood, and hard boiled eggs added to the softfood.

THE AVIARY YEAR

January

This is a quiet month but there are still a few major shows to attend. This is also probably the last chance to buy any birds required for the breeding season.

Most breeders will have disposed of any surplus birds by now but it can be a good time to get good quality birds because breeders may decide to sell one or two of the better quality birds that they have kept just in case they lost any of their stock through the winter.

I give no extra food other than a basic seed mix and fresh water. In my experience, it is better to let the birds have a hard month. I do not starve them, but I cut things down considerably.

This is a good time to do all maintenance jobs. The bird room and particularly cages benefit from a bit of attention.

Remember to order rings early for your straight breeding pairs of British birds. This applies especially to anyone who is planning to breed crossbills as, by this time, you should already be getting ready to prepare the nesting sites.

The rings you require can be purchased from the British Bird Council (see the section on ringing, page 131). These rings must be fitted when the young are approximately five days old, although this varies from species to species and depends on how well the young are being fed.

Young mules and finches grow very quickly so be careful not to miss ringing them. Many a good bird has been bred but could not be exhibited or sold because the breeder missed ringing it.

February

This is just about your last chance to place mule and hybrid pairs together before they get too fit. I even pair up some of my birds as early as December because they will be less trouble if they are well accustomed to each other before the breeding season begins.

When two birds are put together, you should always provide two water and seed pots. That should be maintained until you see both birds eating from the same pot. This helps to prevent a lot of squabbling. Now is the time to dose the birds with their first course of vitamins.

All maintenance to cages should have been completed. If you require any birds to complete your breeding plans then this is probably the last chance you will have to acquire them.

Towards the end of the month, my pairs are put into bigger cages, especially my hens. This helps to remove any fat and starts to bring them into condition.

At the end of February, if you want to rear a nest of canaries first, before your finches come into condition, put the canary pair and the finch cock together. If squabbling occurs, put the hen in the middle of a treble breeding cage with the canary cock on one side and the finch on the other. The sliding dividers should be made of wire mesh so that the birds can see each other. This will prevent the canary hen laying a round of clear eggs before the finch comes into condition.

I personally do not use this approach, preferring to leave my muling pairs together so that they bond and get used to only one mate. Later in the season I occasionally split pairs that have not bonded. Some pairs are just incompatible, so as a last resort I will split up these pairs and try them with other birds and occasionally this approach works.

March

Now is the time to cut the birds' claws. Cock and hen Norwich canaries' vents are washed and trimmed, being careful not to trim the 'feeler' feathers. If you blow the bird's feathers away from the body in the vent region, you will clearly see the long feathers around the vent. These are the feeler feathers which help during copulation and must not be touched.

Cages should be thoroughly cleaned as this will be the last time you will be able to clean them thoroughly until the breeding season ends. All birds and cages should be treated with an anti-mite spray.

Feeding is vastly increased during this month. A richer seed mix is supplied. Hard boiled eggs are fed, mixed in with small amounts of egg food every day. On alternate days, greenfood of your choice should be provided. A good supply of grit should be available, plus more vitamins. Small amounts of livefood can be offered to finches that require them for rearing, such as chaffinches and bramblings. Siskins, redpolls and bullfinches will also eat livefood even though it is not essential.

Lesser redpoll pair

Nest boxes and bowls should now be prepared. The birds in a pair should be separated for the two weeks at the end

of March. If solid dividers are used, a small gap should be left through which the cock and hen can feed each other, without gaining access to the other half of the cage. No gap need be left if the dividers are wire mesh. This separation may not be necessary if a pair has already formed a strong bond and are feeding each other.

April

The nest sites and nest material should be made available in April. The exceptions are crossbills as their breeding season is two months in front of the other birds (see January). Crossbills should already have young and could possibly be on their second round.

For the rest, continue to feed the same as in March. If the birds in a pair have been kept apart, reintroduce them by the end of April. Any pairs that do not seem interested in breeding should be split up again for another week or so. Keep in mind that some species do not come into breeding condition until May. Goldfinches are always later but greenfinches are early nesters.

I find that most domesticated British birds come into condition about a month earlier than their wild counterparts. Canaries, by this time, should be chipping their first

Twite mule with canary foster parents

clutch and if you have already earmarked any for muling, now is the time to try to reintroduce the finch cock. If he helps with feeding and does not interfere with nest or chicks, leave him there. If it looks as though he might be disruptive, insert a wire slide and keep him away from the nest. When the canary hen is ready to go to nest again, let him in with the hen in the morning and again at night.

Eggs should be removed early every morning and replaced with dummies. The eggs can be put under foster pairs, so that they can rear the chick. I usually foster out only half of the eggs in the first round. This gives me a better chance of rearing at least some chicks and it also proves whether my breeding pairs will rear their own. I personally prefer to leave a finch with its canary even if the canary's first round of eggs is clear. After the canary hen has incubated for 14 days the eggs can be thrown away and early finch cocks, like greenfinches, linnets and redpolls, are ready and more likely to fertilise eggs. Leaving the finch with the canary also stops the canary from pair bonding with another bird. If that happens, this new bond can sometimes be difficult to break. Then, at least half the season, if not all, is wasted.

May

By May you should have some young but you will probably also have plenty of hard luck stories and several nightmares. This is the time when months of planning sometimes have to go in the bin and you start again. That's the

Baby with full crop

bad news. The good news is that it's not too late. Some of your plans will not have gone as expected. A cock in one cage will be displaying to a hen in another, or a hen will not have anything to do with her chosen mate. Now is the time to split the pair and try new mates.

17 day-old goldfinches

Swapping things around might result in breeding something you hadn't planned for, but it is better to breed something rather than nothing at all. And you may be pleasantly surprised. There have been occasions when making a change in May has produced a breeder's best bird of the season.

The secret of successful breeding lies in watching the birds carefully. Do not interfere too soon or keep swapping and changing. But do not be afraid to do so if things

An incompatible pair

go wrong or if a pair seems totally incompatible. Young birds should be moved from their parents as soon as they are eating well enough to be sure that they are capable of supporting themselves. This is usually at about 24 days.

I house my youngsters in family groups to upset them as little as possible when moving them. I always put my young finches and mules on a sulpha drug (such as sulphadimidine or sulphamethadine) until they have completed their first moult to protect them from going light.

Such drugs are available from a vet. Your vet will ask you to take a sick bird for him to see. Do not be put off. Just put any greenfinch in a cage and take it along to his surgery. Tell him that you don't have any sick birds, yet, but that you need this drug as a preventative measure. Most vets will then supply you with the appropriate drug as often as you require, on repeat prescription, without asking to see any birds.

Going light or weight loss is a symptom of lankesterellosis or coccidiosis. These diseases are caused by protozoal parasites in the gastrointestinal systems of the birds. The parasites build up in young birds, especially greenfinches, until the bird wastes away and dies. Sulpha-based drugs do not cure the illness, but keep it at bay until the young bird's immune system can handle it. Each species of the coccidia parasite is host specific which means only greenfinches are vunerable to one type and linnets to another and so on. Drug treatment should be continued until the end of the bird's first moult after which it can be stopped.

Unfortunately, the problem never goes completely away as the adult birds pass on the protozoa to their young every year and so the cycle continues. Twenty years ago, lots of aviary-bred birds used to die and many breeders stopped keeping greenfinches. Since the parasite has been better understood, and sulpha-based drugs have been used, hardly any birds are lost from going light.

June

By June, or sometimes even earlier, you should have young ready to bolt the nest. If the hen starts to carry nest material, provide her with a new nest site and nesting material. Otherwise, she may try to lay in the old nest. If she does, just remove the eggs as normal and replace them with dummies. Wait until she is fully broody before replacing the clutch. This will help stop the young from destroying the eggs or disturbing the hen.

If necessary swap the eggs with a clutch from a proven foster pair. Then, if you wish, you can return the eggs to the hen that laid them once the young have been removed to their new housing. When the young are split from their parents they should be given soak seed, egg food and fresh greens at least twice a day.

At the end of June, it is wise to begin colour feeding any youngsters of seven or eight weeks. This is essential if you intend to exhibit them, though I colour feed all my mules and hybrids whether they are of show quality or not.

Birds do change when they have moulted and you could miss colour feeding a potential show bird if you do not start to colour feed early enough. Birds look better when they have been colour fed so even the birds you eventually dispose of will be more attractive to buyers if they have been colour fed. With certain species, colour feeding also assists in sexing youngsters.

Geenfinch hen with yellow Norwich cock

July

This is probably the busiest month in the year. You will have young and eggs, some birds moulting and others weaning. If you are having a good year, every cage will be bursting at the seams. If you were to hit a really lucky streak there would be yellow mule cocks everywhere, rare hybrids, 50 unflighted yellow Norwich hens, no buff cocks and enough young feeders to replace the older pairs!

The following year you would be quite self sufficient, with no need to bring in new stock. It is wonderful thought but sadly exists only in dreams. If only breeding mules was that easy.

A more likely scenario is that by this time the birds will be getting tired and you will be more tired that the birds. If you are having a bad breeding season you could be getting rather fed up with all the hard work. The lawn needs cutting and the house needs painting and you really need a holiday. But keep going. There is not long to go.

This is the time when you may just breed that one hybrid you have been dreaming of. This is the month when the unexpected can, and often does, happen, so see it through.

If pairs have really done well for you and bred two or three rounds of young then now is the time to split them. Take one last clutch of eggs and let the feeder canaries rear them.

August

By August all of the pairs should have been split up and be in full moult. The moult normally takes about seven or eight weeks to complete. Adult birds will replace every feather but a young bird will moult its body and head feathers but not its main flight feathers or tail. That is why they are called unflighted. Next year, after they have moulted their flight feathers, they will be called flighted.

Colour feeding should be well under way. I use Carophyll Red, which is a red powder. I put one and a half level mustard spoonfuls in a one litre plastic bottle and pour some boiling water on it. I leave that for 24 hours then top up the bottle with cold water. The water should then be a rich red in colour.

This solution is then given to all the birds you want to colour feed. Do not feed it to green birds – such as greenfinches and siskins but do give it to brown birds like redpolls, linnets, goldfinches and bullfinches. You can even give it to bullfinch hens. They will not turn red but their body colour will look richer and the black will take on a rich sheen. Colour feeding goldfinches will change the yellow wing feathers to orange. I personally prefer them to be yellow so I don't colour feed goldfinches until only their heads are left to moult. Mostly I don't bother to colour feed them at all. Colour feeding your finches is really only necessary if your birds are to be shown although it does enhance their natural colour and makes them more attractive.

Norwich canaries look better when colour fed. Because

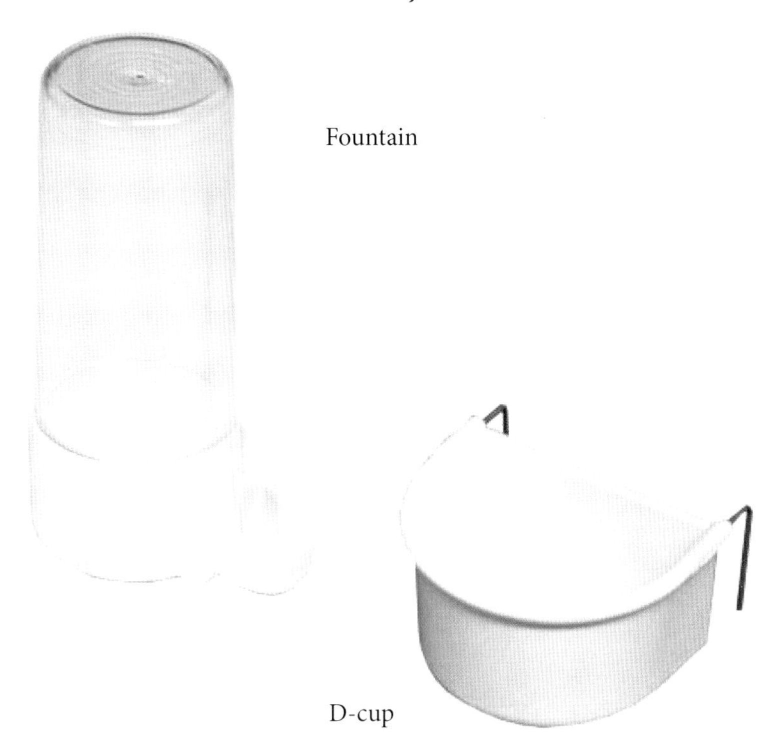

young birds do not moult the wing and tail feathers, these feathers will show no colour. When buying birds this is the best proof that the birds you are buying are current year bred. All your mules, whatever their finch parentage, should be colour fed.

I use plastic water fountains at this time. As the day goes on the colour food settles and the colour is much ricer at the bottom, which is where the birds drink from. So with a water fountain the birds take more colour food. If you use 'D' cup drinkers, the colour food still has a tendency to sink to the bottom and the birds drink the clear water from the top. Even though I use fountains, I shake them halfway through the day to remix the colour food.

Regular baths are essential

September

It is best not to disturb birds too much in September, when they are in the moult. Make baths available regularly, but do not leave them on the cage, in case the birds drink this water and not the colour food. If that happens the birds' coloration will be patchy.

The colour food mixture must remain constant all through the moult until the colour reaches the head and just the head is left to moult. You can then reduce the strength of the colour food mixture to half the original strength.

Regular spraying is advisable at this time as it helps to prevent the new feathers from coming through dry and brittle. It also helps the birds have a quick and easy moult.

Continue to give your birds extra vitamins and minerals and greenfood as moulting takes a lot out of the birds.

By the end of this month, the need to sweep up feathers should begin to decrease and most birds should be back on plain water.

You will start to be able to identify the good and not-so-good birds that the season has produced. This can be the best time of the year. If you have no young birds showing any promise, it can be worst time.

October

October is the month when you can start to sort out the birds that you want to show or keep. It is also the time to prepare for your first show. The birds you intend to show should be separated from the rest, kept in clean cages and given baths daily.

It is wise to keep them on colour food so that when the odd feather is dropped, its replacement will be coloured. Any late bred youngsters will still be on colour food as they do not moult until they are six weeks old and the moult lasts for another six or seven weeks. The birds that you intend to show this season should be kept on half strength colour food because these birds may drop the occasional feather and replacement feathers need to be the same colour. Odd feathers can be dropped for various reasons; catching birds up for a show, transporting them, sudden surprises at a show or a noisy bonfire night. Young birds are always more inclined to be nervous than over-year birds.

It is a good idea to begin show training by giving the birds access to a training cage. Fix training cages to the outside of the cage so that its open door lines up with the open door of the stock cage. Put attractive tit bits of food, for example a sprig of greenfood, in the training cage to encourage the birds to go in.

If the training cages are all wire the birds soon get used

to them, and like to be in them because they can see all round. Then, when you rattle a stick in the stock cage the birds will go straight into the show cage to escape your attentions. You can then put the show cage on a shelf while you tend the rest of the birds.

The final part of a bird's training is to take it to a local show. A one day event is ideal, so that the birds don't have far to travel and are only out for one day. All birds benefit from this training.

November

November is the month the major British bird shows begin. These shows are spread all over the country so the birds have to be used to travelling. Also the time the birds are out of the shed can extend to a couple of days, so training done at smaller shows will now pay dividends.

This is the time when the mules or hybrids you have bred will now earn their keep. If your intention is to exhibit them, do not worry if in their first year they do not win top prizes. The main thing is to have them in the competition. Mules and hybrids get better each year.

If you are fortunate enough to win best unflighted awards this year the competition will get much harder next year. First-year birds need only beat other first-year birds, but when they have to be shown in the adult classes they will come up against the best birds that have been bred for a number of years.

Always remember that not every bird can win. Even the top breeders lose sometimes, but that makes the occasions when you win even more special.

December

By December the weather is getting colder. At this time

of year I heat my bird room a little. I use an electric, thermostatically-controlled, greenhouse heater which does not use vast amounts of electricity, particularly as I keep it set at frost level.

The amount of heat it provides just stops the water pots from freezing but it never actually warms the room. I find that although the cold itself does the birds no damage, not having constant access to water is harmful. Without the heater, I would be defrosting water pots all day during a cold spell.

If the weather turns really cold, I feed extra fatty foods including suet and groats. I do not offer large quantities, just the occasionally tit bit. Very little greenfood is fed during December. A small piece of broccoli, perhaps once or twice a week, does no harm, but the diet other than that, is kept very plain.

There is little else to do in the bird room during December, other than maintenance and shows. This is just as well because Christmas keeps most of us busy enough, without having to spend hours in the bird room.

Hybrids can get very aggressive

Goldfinch × bullfinch family

EPILOGUE

I hope sincerely that this book helps you in your bird keeping. I believe all bird keepers should do their bit by passing on the knowledge that they have gained from practical experience, so that newcomers to this rewarding hobby might avoid repeating our mistakes.

It is my firm belief that all fanciers should put more into the hobby than they take out. If it wasn't for the bird fanciers who run shows and clubs throughout the year, the fancy would cease to be. It is these people who keep our hobby strong and who will make sure it continues to be strong long into the future.

It is a wonderful hobby through which I have met thousands of interesting people and made many life-long friends. If this book, which is my latest project within the world of bird keeping, encourages only one new person to take up this fantastic hobby, then the hundreds of hours it has taken will be worthwhile.

Whilst completing this section I received a telephone call telling me of the death of a great friend and wonderful bird man, Victor Carr. Victor was the gentleman of our hobby, founder member of the British Bird Council, one of the best administrators the British bird fancy has been fortunate enough to have, author of two books on mules and hybrids and much more. It was a very sad day for the hobby. Luckily, his knowledge will not be lost and his name will never be forgotten. His books will guarantee that.

You will have seen when reading this book I have included pictures of a few people that I won't be seeing at shows anymore. Every year we seem to lose someone from our hobby and in the last few years we have lost some great characters, both top breeders and exhibitors. I will name just a few who have been close friends and whose experience in the hobby will be sadly missed: Derek Oldknow, Peter Lander, Baz Morris, Peter Bailey, Larret Franks, John Broadbent, Lyn Jones and Grosvenor Ridgeway. I wish that these people had written down all their experiences. They would have made a great read and have been invaluable sources of information to beginners and champions alike.

The late Victor Carr with a hawfinch in 1972 that was shown under licence

ABOUT THE AUTHOR

(Adapted from Ron Toft's 1999 article
for the *National Exhibition Show Catalogue*.)

There cannot be many people in British avicultural circles who don't know or haven't heard of Bernard Williams. Since 1959, Bernard, who is in his early 50s and lives in Staffordshire, has been involved in, and excelled at, practically every aspect of bird keeping. He has been a breeder, an exhibitor, a trader, a judge, a collector, a club founder, a club official and a source of invaluable knowledge which he has readily imparted to anyone willing to listen. But if there is one thing that has made Bernard a household name it is his long association with the National Cage & Aviary Birds Exhibition and his work as Show Manager.
Bernard's fascination – no, obsession – with birds began in the 50s as a lad growing up in Staffordshire. 'My father was interested in birds but never actually kept any at that time,' he told me over one of several cups of tea at his home. Bernard didn't see much of his coalminer father when he was a small boy. 'At night he worked down the pits and during the day he was in bed. Sunday was the only day I saw my father. That was when we would pack some sandwiches and a bottle of water and head for the countryside.'

They had to walk a good five miles through row after row of terraced houses before they even set eyes on a tree. 'We just kept going, trying to see as many wild birds as possible. If I spotted a bird I hadn't seen before, such as a tree creeper, that was the highlight of my day,' said Bernard.

Bernard also took great delight in trying to find nests

and marvelled at the different sizes and colours of the eggs they contained. Although he readily admits he collected eggs in a small way (now completely illegal, of course), he never took more than one from each nest. 'It was just a passing phase, something I did while walking.' His main interest was not in nests or eggs but in the birds that made them. 'I wanted to know everything about birds and to see them close-up. There was only one way I could do that – and that was to keep them.'

Living in a small house meant there was no room for a shed or aviary, so Bernard kept his first birds, pigeons, in a small hutch. Then his father introduced him to a friend of his, Ray Bryan, who kept border canaries. 'Most Saturdays, I would be put on a bus and met seven miles down the road by Ray who took me to his house. I would spend the afternoon in awe, helping him and being educated in the art of bird keeping.'

Eventually, Bernard made a cage for a pair of red factor canaries which he kept in his bedroom. 'I bred quite a few birds during the first year. Every morning at first light, I would be awakened by the cock singing merrily and the hen feeding its young. I would lay there for hours just watching them.' One of the first priorities for Bernard when he left home at 19 was building his own shed and aviary. 'I had it up and running within six months, I started keeping canaries of various types as well as some British finches.'

He also joined his local club, Hanley CBS, and within a year became secretary. 'I discovered that administration was my forte. It's not everybody's cup of tea, but it's something I've always enjoyed and it helped prepare me for the rigours, many years later, of managing the National.'

Bernard ran Hanley CBS for 20 years. 'At our best show

Staffordshire British Bird & Mule Club Show held at St Josephs

we had around 1,800 birds. As the fancy declined in the late 70s and early 80s so the number of entries fell to only 800 or 900. In those days there were seven clubs in this area which meant there was a members' show somewhere every Saturday. Sometimes you would have two shows a mile apart on the same day. It was ridiculous. I got all the secretaries together and between us we decided for the good of the fancy locally to reduce the number of shows and incorporate members' events into open shows.'

Bernard also felt the time was right for a specialist mule society in his part of the country, so he invited about 40 people to a meeting and formed the Staffordshire British Bird and Mule Club. 'We had 350 birds at our first show which, by a strange coincidence, was held at the end of the road where I now live. Later we had to find a bigger venue and eventually attracted 750 entries. The club is still going strong. And in 2002, I was asked to judge the club's show, which was very nice. I've judged at most of the major shows and feel very honoured to have also been asked to judge again at the National British Bird and Mule Club Show. In 2004, I was also asked to join the committee.'

National British Bird & Mule Club Show, Winsford Civic Hall

Bernard's involvement with the National dates back to the late 60s when he was an exhibitor. After he stopped showing he became a trader selling a wide range of ceramic trophies. 'I used to be a self employed engineer, repairing and maintaining machinery in ceramic factories in Stoke-on-Trent. I began looking at the products made in these factories in an avicultural light, thinking: wouldn't that particular item look lovely with a picture of a bird on it? Many bird show trophies around then were made of plastic. I decided to commission a range of ceramic ones which I sold. They went down extremely well, partly because they could be taken home and displayed as nice ornaments in their own right.'

Realising the potential, Bernard had more ceramic trophies made and began selling them far and wide, eventually giving up

his engineering job and devoting most of his time to marketing and manufacturing these specially-made products.

'At one point I was supplying 500 societies around the world,' said Bernard. 'I ran that business for about 10 years. I then had two slipped discs and didn't walk for a year. During that time, I ran the operation from a bed in the living room. I was told I would never walk again, but I proved them wrong. Nevertheless, I decided to sell the business as a going concern. Having my own trade stand at the National for about 10 years gave me invaluable experience in a completely different aspect of aviculture, one which most bird keepers never get to see.'

Bernard later became a British section representative at the National, then Assistant Show Manager and finally Show Manager; a job he carried out with aplomb for about five years and which occupied about four months of his time every year.

'Having run a large cage bird society and having started a specialist club and seeing that become one of the biggest such clubs in the country, I suppose I considered the ultimate advancement would be running the National. But I never, ever dreamed I would end up doing just that. Being asked to be Show Manager is a bit like being appointed Manager of the England football team. It's the biggest honour ever bestowed on me.'

Running the National was hard, often frustrating, work. 'There were so many dimensions to the National and new problems constantly arose. Take the 2003 show as an example. For the first time, the local authority banned smoking in that part of the NEC where the show was held. That was a condition of the licence. Smoking had never been an issue before. In the past, we erected 'No smoking' signs and hoped that visitors would respect the request. It was a very difficult thing to enforce, given the wide range of people who attend the National. I knew full well that some people might take the view that if

National Exhibition
NEC Birmingham
1993

they could not smoke, they would no longer attend the show. Personally, and speaking as a smoker, I felt that a greater degree of flexibility would have benefitted the show.'

'However, we would not have been granted the licence had we not agreed to the ban. It was my job to enforce this rule, and enforce it I did. Fortunately, the vast majority of smokers were not put off and those who attended co-operated. I use that example to demonstrate that there is far more to running a show as large as the National than just putting cages on staging.'

Bernard's first love is British mules and hybrids. 'I think that came from being out in the countryside so much when I was young. Not living in a town, I had never seen a canary and only a few budgies, which didn't particularly appeal to me. The first birds I saw were wild birds. In fact, if bird-keeping, God forbid, were to be banned tomorrow, I would become a bird-watcher or bird photographer. That's the extent of my passion, my obsession with all things feathered.'

Bernard has kept all sorts of British birds over the years – from thrushes to finches. 'I particularly like the twite and kept quite a few breeding twite mules for a number of years. I bred 14 or 15 one season, achieved what I had set out to do and moved on to another species.' Moving on has characterised much of Bernard's bird keeping. 'I keep a species or variety not to show but to learn as much as possible about it – everything from courtship and mating to song and feeding habits. Once I've learned as much as possible I generally move on to another species and start all over again. Personally I've never wanted to specialise in just one species and keep only, say, greenfinches and goldfinches.'

Bernard says that anyone can breed a mule, a cross between a canary and a British bird, but the problems really start when large good quality Norwich canaries are used. 'A potentially show-winning mule has to be bred from a Norwich and what you need are pure yellow canary cocks and hens. Norwich cocks are muled with finch hens and Norwich hens are muled with finch cocks. Buffs are no good. Neither is an otherwise perfect bird with a white tail feather. You are constantly replacing your stock and all the time trying to produce better and better quality mules.'

Bernard has about 100 birds at present, the majority being Norwich and Fife canaries. His finches and hybrids include crossbills, bramblings, bullfinches, goldfinches, greenfinches, chaffinches and redpolls. He tends not to breed so many finches at present, preferring instead to obtain whatever he needs from finch-breeding friends. 'You need to specialise in finches,' said Bernard. 'Luckily I've got quite a few friends who supply me with the odd finch cock. Such birds are of far better quality than anything I could produce because I would have to keep 10 pairs of a particular finch to get one that would be good enough for hybridising. It's easier to go to a top-line finch breeder.'

Yellow siskin × canary cock

In January 2003, Bernard doubled the size of his 12ft × 10ft bird room because he felt the original was too claustrophobic. 'I wanted more natural light, more room in which to move about and space for a sink.' He drew up the plans, had the bird room extended by a contractor and then built and fitted all the cages himself. 'In my early 50s there is no way now I am going to pack up keeping birds. I really felt it was about time I had a shed that was not only comfortable for my birds but also comfortable for me.'

Although Bernard has outdoor aviaries, nowadays he prefers to keep most of his birds inside in large cages and breeding pens. 'My birds have the best of everything, are not exposed to adverse weather conditions and are not at risk from vermin and predators. What's more I can see all my birds close up whereas, in large aviaries, they can be difficult to observe. Having said that, my aviaries are useful. Some species will not breed in small pens, and large aviaries help to get birds fit and ready for the breeding season. Also there is nothing nicer than seeing birds in captivity but having so much freedom.'

He believes that to breed all the species of British bird and their hybrids successfully, requires a varied selection of accommodation in sizes to suit all species.

I asked Bernard if bird keeping still held the same fascination for him now as it did when he started. He replied: 'For me birds are more than a fascination. They are an obsession. Although I know a lot about most British species there is still more to learn. I like nothing better than soaking up new information, also there are so many different avenues one can go down. One of my current favourites is the history of bird keeping around the world. The hobby has been good to me, that's why I help beginners as much as possible. It's important to try to put back more than you take out, to help the next generation and lay foundations for the future.'